WILLIAM CAREY.

SERAMPORE LETTERS

BEING THE UNPUBLISHED CORRESPONDENCE OF
WILLIAM CAREY AND OTHERS WITH
JOHN WILLIAMS

1800-1816

EDITED BY

LEIGHTON AND MORNAY WILLIAMS

WITH AN INTRODUCTION BY

THOMAS WRIGHT

G. P. PUTNAM'S SONS

NEW YORK   LONDON
27 WEST TWENTY-THIRD STREET   24 BEDFORD STREET, STRAND

The Knickerbocker Press

1892

Copyright, 1892
BY
LEIGHTON AND MORNAY WILLIAMS

Electrotyped, Printed, and Bound by
The Knickerbocker Press, New York
G. P. Putnam's Sons

PREFACE.

THE introduction of Mr. Wright presents very clearly the English setting of the letters included in this collection, and the notes which have been interspersed among them give sufficient explanation to form a continuous narrative. A word, however, may be premised here as to the special interest of the letters in connection with the centennial of the Baptist Missionary Society.

The letters throw a new and unexpected light on the American connection with the Serampore Mission of the English Baptists. The obstacles placed in the way of the English missionaries by the East India Company made it necessary for them to make the voyage by way of America, and they were thrown on the hospitality of their American brethren. A regular correspondence thus sprang up between the society at home and the Serampore missionaries, carried on from this country mainly by Dr. William Rogers, of Philadelphia, and the Rev. John Williams, of New York. A warm friendship seems thus to have grown up between the brethren on both sides of the sea, a friendship which, in the providence of God, proved of no little benefit to the Baptists in this country. The letters furnish also important evidence of indebtedness to the English brethren in the commencement of work in America, as will be seen by the letter from William Carey to John Williams announcing the conversion of Judson to Baptist views. The letters have a third source of interest in the evidence which they afford of the active missionary sympathies and efforts of the New York churches at this early period. The credit of the formation of the Missionary Union has hitherto been given almost exclusively to the Baptists of Massachusetts; but it will appear from these records that the earliest missionary society in this country was formed in New York City, and that of that Society John Williams was a Director and Dr. Carey a correspondent. Before the date of Judson's departure for India a Baptist Society had also been formed in this city in connection with the Baptist Association; and even before the formation of the Society the Association itself had supported the Rev. Elkanah Holmes as a missionary to the Indians. In this work of Mr. Holmes, Carey seems to have felt the deepest interest. When the Baptist Missionary Society was formed in New York, John Williams became its first president, and John Cauldwell, a deacon of his church, was elected its treasurer, and later the first treasurer of the

Missionary Union. We have thus the evidence of a share in the origin of the Missionary Union on the part of the New York brethren fully as large as that rightly claimed by those in Boston. But after all, perhaps the chief interest of the letters to the general reader will be found in the vivid portraiture which they bring before us of the man to whom, under God, the work of modern missions is most largely indebted, as his character is presented unconsciously to himself in the thoughts and feelings to which he gives expression in these letters to a friend whom he had never seen, but whom he knew to to be like-minded in faith and purpose. From the example which they afford of wide, unselfish interest, and a firm, unshaken faith and determination, we may well glean lessons of the highest value to ourselves, as well as a juster appreciation of the narrow resources and deep draughts on faith out of which this great work has grown.

Our grateful acknowledgments are due to the friends who have aided in this compilation, especially to Thomas Wright, Esq., and to Sir William Thomas Lewis.

It is proper to state that the letters are given as they were written, and that in all cases the spelling of native names has been left unchanged.

ILLUSTRATIONS.

INTRODUCTION.

THE EARLY DAYS OF THE GREAT MISSIONARY MOVEMENT.

THE year 1892, the centenary of the foundation of the Baptist Missionary Society, is a fitting time to take some note of the humble twig from which has sprung the magnificent growth of Foreign Missions—a growth, moreover, which, notwithstanding its noble proportions, is as nothing compared with that vastness whereunto, under God, it will doubtless hereafter attain.

To whom belongs the honor of first pressing the claims of the heathen on the Christianity of this country it is difficult to say, but it must be remembered that in the spring of the year 1784, at a meeting of the Northamptonshire Baptist churches, it was agreed, on the motion of the Rev. John Sutcliff of Olney, to set apart an hour on the evening of the first Monday in

1

every month for social prayer for the success of the Gospel, and to invite Christians of other denominations to unite with them in it. The measure thus recommended was eagerly adopted by great numbers of the churches, and so marked a revival of religion ensued that it was afterwards regarded by the associated ministers and the missionaries as the actual commencement of the Missionary movement.

The Rev. John Sutcliff, who was born at a place called Straithey, near Hebden Bridge, Yorkshire, in 1752, was trained for the ministry at Bristol College, then under the care of the Revs. Hugh and Caleb Evans. A paper containing " a view " of Mr. Sutcliff's studies during one year, and the letter in which, when about to leave college, he thanks his tutors for " all favours conferred upon him," are in the possession of Sir William Thomas Lewis. Mr. Sutcliff was tall of stature, being over six feet; and another distinctive feature of his personal appearance was a very decided Roman nose, which was responsible for several amusing anecdotes. A Baptist minister of my acquaintance relates them with great unction, but as so much depends upon the way they are told, I shall make no attempt to reproduce them here. Mr. Sutcliff lived in a large house adjoining the chapel. It was owned by and the residence of a Mrs. Andrews, a member of his congregation. The house is still standing, though much altered. A stone near the roof is thus cut:

SUTCLIFF'S HOUSE, OLNEY.

It was in 1776, at an association meeting at Olney, that Sutcliff became acquainted with Andrew Fuller, and they were fast friends during the rest of their lives. Born in 1754 at Wicken, near Ely, Fuller, who was thus two years Mr. Sutcliff's junior, had, in 1775, been ordained to the pastorate of the church at Soham. But both he and his people were "very unhappy. The place was truly a Bochim!" Three of the letters written by Fuller to Sutcliff are in the possession of Sir W. T. Lewis. In one, dated 13th of March, 1781, Fuller "admires" Sutcliff's "thoughts on divine Jealousy," and happily remarks, in connection with the importance of searching the Scriptures : "We have undoubtedly many excellent bodies of Divinity extant, but none perfect. Notwithstanding the numerous and elaborate productions of the pious and the wise through successive ages, scripture still remains and will remain an unexplored deep." On August 15th of the same year Fuller wants Sutcliff's thoughts on the question : *In what manner may we now unwarrantably expect divine direction ?* In another letter he recommends his friend to "Read the Bible, not with a system before your

eyes, but as a little child, with humility and prayer " ;
and Sutcliff's letters in reply were in a similar strain.
In 1782 Fuller removed from "Bochim" to Kettering,
where he found himself separated from his friend Sutcliff, and also from another of his friends, Ryland of
Northampton, by only a few miles.

For the furtherance of his motion of 1784 Sutcliff in
1789 republished Jonathan Edwards' work entitled
"An humble attempt to promote explicit agreement
and visible union of God's people in Extraordinary
Prayer," which, according to the title-page, was
"Printed at Boston in New England 1747, Reprinted at
Northampton in Old England 1789." After stating
that he does not consider himself answerable for every
statement the book contains, Mr. Sutcliff concludes his
preface in the following beautiful manner : " In the
present imperfect state we may reasonably expect a
diversity of sentiments upon religious matters. Each
ought to think for himself ; and every one has a right
on proper occasions to show his opinion. Yet all
should remember there are but two parties in the world,
each engaged in opposite causes ; the cause of God and
of Satan ; of holiness and sin ; of heaven and hell.
The advancement of the one and the downfall of the
other must appear exceedingly desirable to every real
friend of God and man. If such, in some respects, entertain different sentiments and practise distinguishing
modes of worship, surely they may unite in the above

business. Oh for thousands upon thousands divided into small bands of their respective cities, towns, villages, and neighbourhoods, all met at the same time and in pursuit of one end, offering up their united prayers like so many ascending clouds of incense before the most High."

" This publication," says Fuller, " had a very considerable influence in originating that tone of feeling which in the end determined five or six individuals to venture, though with many fears and misgivings, on the mighty undertaking of founding the Baptist Missionary Society."

Our eyes next turn to the remarkable William Carey. Born at Hackleton in Northamptonshire of poor parents in 1761, Carey was at the age of fourteen apprenticed to the shoemaking, and for many years his life was a continuous battle with poverty. Being determined to improve his mind, however, this did not deter him. He got hold of some books and soon we find him studying the Greek Testament. The preaching of the Rev. Thomas Scott and other divines of the neighborhood led him to serious thoughts, and the perusal of a work by the Rev. Robert Hall, senior, convinced him that it was his duty to proclaim to others the Christ he had found for himself. Consequently in the year 1780, when he was only nineteen, he made his appearance in one of the village pulpits, and preached his first sermon.

An important event to Carey was the meeting of the Northamptonshire Baptist Association at Olney in 1782, for then it was that he first heard the Rev. John (Dr.) Ryland preach. The text was "Be not children in understanding." Says Carey : "I, not possessed of a penny, that I recollect, went to Olney. I fasted all day because I could not purchase a dinner ; but towards evening, Mr. Chater, in company with some friends from Earl's Barton saw me, and asked me to go with them, where I remember I got a glass of wine." Previously Carey had been attached to the Established Church, but during this period his views on the subject of baptism changed, and accordingly he was immersed by Dr. John Ryland in October, 1783. Having now become intimate with the Rev. John Sutcliff, Carey began to show himself more frequently at Olney, and by and by joined Mr. Sutcliff's church, his chief reason for doing so being because he could not see with the people of Hackleton, who were hyper-Calvinists. After his name in the Hackleton church-book are the words—

"Went away without his dismission."

Mr. Sutcliff put a Latin grammar into his hand, and through his help Carey began to read the Scriptures in Greek and Hebrew.

There are six entries relating to Carey in the Baptist church-book at Olney. The first relates to his admis-

sion to the church there, and the last to his dismission
to the church at Moulton in Northamptonshire, of which
he became minister in 1787. He had for some time
been married, and a young family was growing up
around him, consequently seeing that his congregation
could only raise him £16 a year, it was necessary to
keep on with the shoemaking as well. For a time, too,
he kept a school, and it was while perusing *Cook's
Voyages* and teaching his pupils geography that the
great project of his life was formed, for no sooner had
he become acquainted with the spiritual degradation of
the heathen than he felt desirous of communicating
the Gospel to them. As he sat in his little workshop he
turned his eyes every now and then towards a large map
suspended on the wall, on which he had rudely repre-
sented the spiritual condition of the various countries,
and as much information as he had been able to gather
regarding the national characteristics and the popula-
tion. In this workshop, as Mr. Wilberforce afterwards
said in the House of Commons, the poor cobbler formed
the resolution to give to the millions of Hindoos the
Bible in their own language.

Very few of Carey's ministerial friends gave him any
encouragement, but among those few was one who was
a host in himself, namely, the Rev. Andrew Fuller.

When Mr. Fuller first heard Carey's proposal he was
so startled by the novelty and magnitude of it that his
feelings resembled those of the infidel courtier in Israel

who cried, "If the Lord should make windows in heaven might such a thing be?"

At a meeting of ministers held about this time at Northampton, Carey suggested as a topic for discussion, the duty of Christians to attempt the spread of the Gospel among the heathen; when Mr. Ryland, senior, sprang to his feet exclaiming, "Young man, sit down! When God pleases to convert the heathen, He will do it without your help or mine!" Neither daunted nor discouraged by repulses, Carey embodied his views in a pamphlet, which he showed to Mr. Fuller, Dr. Ryland, Mr. Sutcliff, and Mr. Pearce of Birmingham, and they advised him to prepare it for publication. Meantime, in spite of his industry—for he still worked at shoemaking,—his family were almost starving; for many weeks they had nothing but bread, and only a scanty supply even of that. Now, in a greater degree than it had ever been, his indomitable energy was in requisition; but difficulties seemed only to spur him onward and he carried everything before him. Neither poverty nor disease, neither the discouraging remarks of his friends nor the unsympathetic conduct of his wife, had any effect on his tenacity of purpose, or if effective at all they only strengthened it.

At first Sutcliff and Fuller had counselled deliberation, but in April, 1791, in their lectures at the Association at Clipstone, they expressed themselves as eager for instant action as was Carey. Both the lectures or sermons bore upon the meditated mission to the heathen, Sutcliff's subject being "Jealousy for God," from I Kings xix., 10.

After the meeting Carey, with almost agonizing earnestness, pressed immediate action, urging that something should be done that very day towards the formation of a society to propagate the Gospel among the heathen.

The ministers recommended him to publish his "Thoughts," and soon afterwards his pamphlet appeared under the title of *An Inquiry into the Obligations of Christians to Send the Gospel to the Heathen.* The next Association was held at Nottingham on the 30th of May, 1792, and Carey was appointed to preach. His sermon on this occasion has ever since been remembered as having laid the foundation of the Baptist Missionary Society. He took for his text : "Enlarge the place of thy tent, and let them stretch forth the curtain of thy habitations. Spare not ; lengthen thy cords and strengthen thy stakes ; for thou shalt break forth on the right hand and on the left ; and thy seed shall inherit the Gentiles and make the desolate cities to be inhabited." From this text he deduced and enforced the two principles which were embodied in the motto of the Mission, "Expect great things ; attempt great things." And such ardor did he put into his discourse, and so ably did he expound his views, that the ministers at length came to the resolution that "a plan should be prepared against the next ministers' meeting for the establishment of a society for propagating the Gospel among the heathen." "If," said Dr. Ryland, "all the people had lifted up their voice and wept as the children of Israel did at Bochim, I should not have wondered at the effect; it would only have seemed proportionate to the cause, so clearly did Mr. Carey prove the criminality of our supineness in the cause of God." At the next meeting, which was held at Kettering on the 2d of October, 1792, in the house (which is still standing) of Mrs. Beeby Wallis, the question of establishing a Missionary Society was discussed; and all objections having been overruled by Mr. Carey's energy, a society was constituted "to convey the message of salvation to some portion of the heathen world." In other words, the Baptist Missionary Society was formed, the first of our great societies that have done so much towards spreading Christianity in foreign lands. The committee of five ministers which was appointed consisted of Andrew Fuller of Kettering, John Ryland of Northampton, John Sutcliff of Olney, Reynold Hogg of Thrapston, and William Carey. The first subscription amounted to £13, 2s. 6d., a surprisingly small sum when we think of the thousands of pounds that have since been collected. And yet, trifling as were the incipient resources, no sooner was the subscription paper filled up than Mr. Carey offered to embark for any country the Society might select.

His mind was fired with enthusiasm, but at the same time he was fully aware that great difficulties would have to be encountered.

Subscriptions now began to come in apace, and the committee soon found themselves in possession of a considerable sum.

The question now was where the proposed Mission should be established. Carey, who had drunk deep draughts from *Cook's Voyages*, thought of Ota-heite ; Pearce, who had been reading about the recent kindness of their king to the shipwrecked crew of the *Antelope*, suggested the Pelew Islands. But just at this moment a gentleman named Mr. Thomas returned from Bengal, who had repeatedly written thence to the leading Baptist ministers in England, giving an account of his conferences with the natives.

"We found," says Dr. Ryland, "that he was now endeavouring to raise a fund for a mission to that country, and to engage a companion to go out with him. It was, therefore, resolved to make some further inquiry respecting him, and to invite him to go back under the patronage of our Society." Although a man of real piety, Mr. Thomas had been " guilty of many faults, many weaknesses, and many failures " ; but the result of the inquiry proved on the whole satisfactory, and it was resolved that Carey and Thomas should proceed to India together.

" It is clear," said Andrew Fuller to Carey, " that

there is a rich mine of gold in India." "And I will go down," returned Carey, "if you will hold the ropes."

The following entries occur in the newly discovered diary of Samuel Teedon, the Olney schoolmaster. The year is 1793 :

"March 24 Sunday ' I went and heard Mr. Storton at Mr. Sutcliff's meeting give a very affecting acct. of the progress of the Gospel among the hindows (= Hindoos) under the ministry of Mr. Thomas and that he and Mr. Cary were to be here and soon embark for their mission after a collection.'

"March 26 Tuesday I went to Mr. Sutcliff's meetg. and heard Mr. Cary preach the Missionary to go to the Hindos (= Hindoos) with his Son about 10 years of age, a collection was made I gave 6*d.* it amounted almost to £10. The Lord prosper the work."

It is deeply interesting to recall this scene in the quaint old meeting-house. The enthusiastic preacher in the tall narrow pulpit against the long back wall ; the cumbrous galleries and the old-fashioned square pews before him crowded with eager listeners—the deep and perpendicular-backed pews with their doors fastened by wooden buttons and their backs of green baize and rows of brass-headed nails ; the large-faced clock whose solemn tickings filled up the pauses in the sermon ; the candles in their wooden blocks dotted about on the tops of the pews ; and the noiseless-footed

BAPTIST CHAPEL AT OLNEY.
(Sutcliff's tomb in left foreground.)

brother, whose duty it was, moving hither and thither with the snuffers. The old chapel is still standing, and has been but little altered.

The sermon which Carey preached, and which poor Samuel Teedon listened to, was from Rom. xii., 1 : " I beseech you, brethren, by the mercies of God, that ye present your bodies a living sacrifice," etc. ; and after the sermon he gave out the hymn commencing—

> " And must I part with all I have,
>   Jesus, my Lord, for Thee ?
> This is my joy, since Thou hast done
>   Much more than this for me "—

pronouncing with great emphasis the first four words of the second verse—

> " *Yes, let it go :*—one look from Thee
>   Will more than make amends
> For all the losses I sustain,
>   Of credit, riches, friends."

All difficulties having been surmounted, Mr. Carey and his family and Mr. Thomas embarked in the *Kron Princessa Maria*, a Danish Indiaman, on the 13th of June, 1793.

The commander of the ship, Captain Christmas, " one of the most polite, accomplished gentlemen, who ever sustained the name of a sea captain," treated them with every kindness. With one of the passengers, a Frenchman, and " the most presumptuous and hardened Deist " he had ever seen or heard of, Carey

engaged in disputes almost daily.   His arguments with
the Frenchman, whose *dernier ressort* was "to turn all
into badinage," availed nothing ; but with the crew,
Danes and Norwegians, amongst whom was "much less
irreligion and profanity" than among English sailors,
he had more success.   Near the Cape the ship got into
such a violent sea that it was thought every moment
she would go to the bottom.   When he thought of his
own "barrenness" and the mighty work that lay
before him, Carey's courage almost failed him, consequently he always felt peculiarly happy during the
times when he knew public worship was going on in
England, and in the reflection that "hundreds if not
thousands" were praying for him.   It is very charac-
teristic of him that in this his first letter from Bengal he
should ask Fuller "to send me all that are published
of Curtis's Botanical Magazine and Sowerby's English
Botany, and to continue sending them regularly, &
deduct what they cost from my allowance."

At Calcutta Carey met with fresh difficulties and
troubles : in the first place, Mr. Thomas, by his imprudence, dissipated their money as soon as it came in ;
again, the government were hostile, and he was in
constant fear lest he should be sent back to England ;
his wife, too, gave him additional trouble, and was
constantly upbraiding him with their wretchedness ;
and, to crown all, his family were attacked by sickness.
Driven almost to distraction by these accumulated

troubles, he removed to the Sunderbunds, where he took a small house and cultivated a piece of land for the support of his family.

Early in 1794 his prospects brightened. He had an invitation to take charge of an indigo factory near Malda, which he reached on the 15th of June ; and here he passed more than five years of his life, free from pecuniary anxieties, preparing himself for more extended labors, and devoting his whole income, after his family had obtained a bare subsistence, to the great cause that lay so near his heart. Had he not worked for his living he and his family would have starved, for the money sent from England, all put together, amounted thus far to only a small sum. Towards the close of 1799 he relinquished his appointment at Malda, where his principal attention had been devoted to the translation of the New Testament into Bengalee, and took up his residence in Serampore, which was in the possession of Denmark.

At home the committee were doing their utmost to serve the Mission, especially Pearce, Fuller, and Sutcliff. On Fuller devolved the duty of traversing the country for funds, on Sutcliff that of preparing fresh students for the Mission field. After his marriage in 1794 Mr. Sutcliff moved from Mrs. Andrews' to the house in the High Street now numbered 21, and this and the next one (No. 23) constituted his seminary. Both houses have since been considerably altered.

Altogether there were thirty-seven students educated at Olney, twelve of whom were specially trained for and entered the Mission field ; and in connection with these labors we have the authority of Mr. Fuller for stating that in all that Mr. Sutcliff did "he saved nothing, but gave his time and talents for the public good."

In May, 1799, Carey was joined by the new missionaries, Marshman, Ward, Brunsdon, and Grant. After a short time Grant, Brunsdon, and Thomas were cut off by death. Grant died on the 31st of October, 1799, Brunsdon on the 3d of July, 1801, Thomas on the 13th of October of the same year. Thus the number of the missionaries was reduced to three, but they were joined in 1802 by another, namely, John Chamberlain, from Mr. Sutcliff's academy at Olney. At Serampore, where they purchased a piece of ground, built a house, and established schools, they received the kindest possible treatment from the governor, Colonel Bie ; indeed, had it not been that Serampore was at that time in the possession of Denmark, and had not the Colonel accorded them his protection, it is very doubtful whether the Mission could have stood its ground—so hostile, at first, were the East India Company and the English government authorities. A boarding-school established by Mr. Marshman had great prosperity and yielded an income of a thousand a year ; and the persistent study of the vernacular languages of India at length brought lucrative employment to Carey. The governor-general, Marquis Wellesley, had taken upon himself the responsibility of founding a college at Fort William, in which the junior servants of the East India Company might undergo a regular course of training for the public service; and his choice fell upon Carey as the most fit person to fill the chair of Professor in the Sanskrit, Bengalee, and Mahratta languages. But it was not the object of the missionaries to make money for themselves; each took for his personal expenses the smallest sum he could, and the rest was devoted to missionary purposes. Out of his income of £1,000 Marshman took for the support of himself and family only £34 a year; Carey, out of his legitimate income of £600, was satisfied with £40 a year; whilst Ward, who did such important service by superintending the printing of the translations that were constantly being issued, would take only £20.

On the 28th of December, 1800, Carey had the privilege of baptizing his first Hindoo convert, Krishnu, who a few days previously had openly renounced his caste, by sitting down at the table of the missionaries. "Thus," says Mr. Ward, "the door of faith is open to the Hindoos, and who shall shut it?"

On the 7th of February, 1801, Carey received from the press the last sheet of the Bengalee New Testament, the fruition of the "sublime thought which he had conceived fifteen years before." The work

2

had been pressed on with such diligence that, in spite of numerous difficulties, it was printed within nine months.

The first convert of the *kayust*, or writer caste, which ranks immediately after that of the Brahmins, was Petumber Sing, baptized at Serampore on the first Sunday in 1802 ; the first Brahmin convert, the amiable and intelligent Krishnu-prisad, who before his baptism trampled on his *poita*, or sacred thread, to indicate his rejection of Hindooism.

In 1803 four more missionaries were ready to embark for India, namely, John Biss, Richard Mardon, William Moore, and Joshua Rowe, all four of whom had been prepared for the Mission field by Mr. Sutcliff at Olney. The British government, however, distrustful of missionary enterprise, had placed so many restrictions on the carriage of missionaries by English ships that it was found better to send the young men first to America, whence they could set sail for India. A letter from the Rev. Andrew Fuller, dated December, 1803, commends them to the Christian hospitality of John Williams, pastor of the Fayette Street church, in New York. " They and their wives," writes Mr. Fuller, " are members of Baptist churches, and have walked as becometh the gospel. Each of the young men has preached in our churches with acceptance." This appeal to the hospitality of the American churches was not made in vain, and not only so, but the visit of the missionaries to New York was the means of causing all earnest Christians of that city to take a real interest in the welfare of the missionary cause, and to help it on in pecuniary and other ways. Thus the interference of the British Government was really a blessing in disguise. The missionaries set out from New York in the ship *Sansom* with a captain who was "quite a gentleman"; on July 4, 1804, they had got as far as Cape Verd Island, and in due time they reached Madras. On the 4th of February, 1805, Moore and Rowe sailed for Bengal, leaving Biss and Mardon to follow them later on. On December 16, 1806, we learn that Biss was down with illness, and it was found that the only way to bring about his recovery was to send him back to England.

"At the beginning of 1804," writes Mr. Marshman, "the missionaries laid before the committee the plans which they had been gradually maturing for the translation and publication of the Scriptures. They stated that there were at least seven languages current in India,—the Bengalee, the Hindoostanee, the Ooriya, the Teloogoo, the Kurnata, the Mahratta, and the Tamul, and they considered it practicable to make a translation of at least the New Testament into some, if not all, of these languages. This proposal exactly coincided with Mr. Fuller's large views, and he introduced it to the public notice by making a tour through the northern counties of England and through Scotland—travelling 1,300 miles and preaching fifty sermons."

The principal portion of the translating was performed by Carey, who, in 1805, published his grammar of the Mahratta language.

In 1806 ground for a mission chapel was purchased in the Lall bazaar in Calcutta, and a temporary bungalow, or thatched house, was erected on it. A chapel was afterwards built on the spot.

In the same year the work that the Lord seemed to have begun in the heart of a Mussulman who lived near Dinagepore gave great delight to Carey, who says: " Whenever he comes to sees us he joins us in family prayer. He lately demolished an Eedgah—a wall with steps along one side of it on which people sit to read the Koran—built many years ago upon his own little estate."

It was Carey's custom to distribute great quantities of tracts every time the people met together to honor " the idol Juggernath, near Serampore." The Brahmins used " to tear them to pieces, and thro' them about the road," but many were carried away by the worshippers, and were the means of doing good.

Among the kind friends who rendered most acceptable aid to the missionaries was Dr. Leyden, the renowned Orientalist, formerly the friend and literary associate of Sir Walter Scott; and Mr. Thomas Manning, the friend of Charles Lamb.

The chief work of Carey's life was the translation of the Scriptures into the languages of the East, and his philological labors were immense. His Mahratta grammar was followed by a Sanscrit grammar in 1806, a Mahratta dictionary in 1810, a Punjabee grammar in 1812, a Telinga grammar in 1814, and a Bengalee dictionary in 1818; these are only a few of the important products of his pen.

While God was blessing the labors of the missionaries abroad, he was prospering the work of the brethren in England. Internal bickerings, which had for some time troubled the denomination, quickly ceased, for people could not fail to see the folly of squabbling over minor differences of religion, when whole continents were without the word of God. The life they sought to impart to India came back in a double life from Heaven to themselves. As Andrew Fuller put it in his letter to Mr. Williams of August 1, 1804, "where any denomination, congregation (or individual) seeks only *its own*, it will be disappointed, but where it seeks the kingdom of God and His righteousness, its own prosperity will be among the things that will be added to it."

Among the passions of his youth that clung to Carey all through his life was the love of flowers—or rather the love of plant life, and we often find him sending to his friends in England for flower seeds or bulbs. His delight on beholding an English daisy springing up, not having seen one for thirty years, is described in one of his letters. It was this incident that gave origin to the well-known lines of James Montgomery, commencing :

"Thrice welcome, little English flower."

Writing to Mr. Williams on November 11, 1801, Carey, after sending his love to a Captain Hague, says : "Tell him when he comes to India again, not to forget his promise to me to furnish the Garden of the Mission House with some American Productions."

In 1806 the New York Baptist Missionary Society is supposed to have been formed, and the Rev. John Williams was the first president.

In 1814 occurred the death of Mr. Sutcliff.

For some time Mr. Sutcliff had been in a declining state of health, but on the 3d of March of that year, whilst on a visit to London, he was seized with a violent pain across his breast and arms, attended with great difficulty of breathing. It took him two days to get home, and it was soon found that the illness was serious.

The last sermon he preached was on Sunday afternoon, February 27th, from Job xiii., 5, 6: "I have heard of Thee by the hearing of the ear," etc. Only once more was he seen in his accustomed place, and that was on one Sunday afternoon in May, when he rode up to the meeting-house to administer the ordinance of the Lord's Supper.

"The last time I visited him," says Mr. Fuller (who frequently during his friend's affliction had ridden over to see him), "was on my way to the annual meeting. Expecting to see his face no more, I said, on taking leave, 'I wish you, my dear brother, an abundant entrance into the everlasting kingdom of our Lord Jesus Christ!' At this he hesitated; not as doubting his entrance into the kingdom, but as questioning whether the term *abundant* were applicable to him. 'That,' said he, 'is more than I expect. I think I understand the connection and import of those words—"Add to your faith virtue—give diligence to make your calling and election sure—for *so* an entrance shall be ministered unto you *abundantly.*" I think the idea is that of a ship coming into harbour with a fair gale and full tide. If I may but reach the heavenly shore, though it be on a board or broken piece of the ship, I shall be satisfied.' "

Andrew Fuller died on May 7, 1815, having survived his friend and fellow-worker only one year. His motto had been that notable verse, Proverbs iii., 6: "In all thy ways acknowledge him, and he shall direct thy paths." With the reliance he had on the wisdom and guidance of God, allied to his own indomitable energy, no wonder he accomplished so much for the great cause that was so near his heart. Almost his last words were, " I wish I had strength enough." " To do what, father? " inquired his daughter. He replied, " To worship, child."

Dr. Carey died on the 9th of June, 1834, in the seventy-third year of his age, and was buried at Serampore.

Meantime a fresh generation of missionaries had sprung up, and among those who continued to preach the Gospel to the heathen were several of Carey's sons. Other bodies of Christians too had founded Missionary societies and sent ministers into various parts of the world. The London Missionary Society was founded in 1795, the Church (of England) Missionary Society in 1799, the Wesleyan Missionary Society in 1817. The interest Americans showed in the good work has already been alluded to, and the agents of their various organizations are still doing, as they did in Carey's time, very effective work in many fields.

THOMAS WRIGHT.

SERAMPORE LETTERS.

A FTER the full and picturesque account, which Mr. Wright has given in his introduction, of the events which led to the sending forth of William Carey and his associates in 1793, it may seem almost unnecessary to add any words as to the men and the district from which they came. And yet, for American readers at least, some little account of the town of Olney may not be amiss. To those accustomed only to the busy, bustling streets of some city in the Western world, Olney would scarcely seem to deserve the name of town, consisting, as it does, for the most part, of one long, broad street, which even its accomplished and ardent eulogist, Mr. Wright, admits to be somewhat deserted ; but in the days when Cowper was living in Olney, and Carey cobbling away in his little shop in the neighboring hamlet of Hackleton, Olney must have been even less an attractive place than it is to-day. Its roads were, if we are to believe William Cowper, by no means desirable ways of traffic and travel, and the long bridge which spanned the marshes between Olney and

Emberton has become classic in our literature for its " wearisome but needful length."

The surroundings of the town of Olney, familiar as they have become to those who love the story of William Cowper and his life, and picturesque as they may appear when in the summer-time the meadows are green with verdure and the hedge-rows bright with flowers, could scarcely have been of the most healthful character ; at least, in the days of which we write. To-day Olney is a healthful and beautiful village according to the estimate of those most competent to judge, but a century ago it was noted for the number of low fevers that were prevalent among its inhabitants, and perhaps the true explanation of that general tone of despondency which marked more than one of John Newton's parishioners is to be found in the malarial character of the surroundings of the town rather than in the moral and intellectual tone of Newton's teaching, which, his enemies said, drove his people mad. Be that as it may, however, it was not a very wealthy nor a very wise community which was embraced within the confines of Olney parish in the closing years of the last century, and yet it is to this little town of Olney that we must look for the men who instituted and who moulded the great missionary movement which has spread to almost every country, and the beneficent results of which can be measured by no statistics of the census gatherer.

THE RIVER OUSE, NEAR OLNEY.

The researches of Mr. Wright have disclosed the fact that in 1672 John Bunyan obtained an indulgence for a meeting to be held in Joseph Kent's barn in Olney, and under this indulgence there came into being the little Christian Church which has come to be known as the Baptist Church in Olney. Of this Church Rev. John Sutcliff became pastor in November, 1775, and, ten years later, William Carey united with the same Church as a member. When Sutcliff commenced his pastorate at Olney, John Newton had been for some eleven years the curate of the parish church of Olney, and, for a somewhat shorter period, the poet, William Cowper, had been an inmate of the tall brick house facing the market-place in Olney, which, while it boasts no special architectural beauties, was then considered the finest house in town. Newton, however, left Olney in 1780, some five years before Carey united with the Baptist Church at Olney, and in 1781, Thomas Scott, the Commentator, succeeded to the curacy of Olney Church. In his charming little work, *The Town of Cowper*, Mr. Wright has pointed out the strange associations that existed between all of these great men, and the way in which John Newton influenced the character of each of the others. Newton, he says, was the bosom friend of Cowper, the spiritual father and friend of Scott, the adviser and warm admirer of Carey, and the kindest relations existed between him and Sutcliff during the five years they were contemporaries at Olney. Yet it was not to John Newton, but to John Sutcliff, that the honor came of being the first of Christian men to propose the setting apart an hour on the evening of the first Monday in each month for social prayer for the success of the Gospel, and to invite Christians of other denominations than his own to unite in it ; and to this suggestion, under God, it may be truly said, is due the inception of modern missions. The way in which the succeeding steps were taken which preceded the sending out of Carey and Thomas on the 13th of June, 1793, have been sufficiently stated by Mr. Wright in his introduction, and without further preface we place before the reader the first letter of the first Missionary of the Baptist Mission Society, written to Andrew Fuller, the first Secretary of that Society :

TO THE SOCIETY FOR THE PROPAGATION OF THE GOSPEL AMONG THE HEATHEN.

BAY OF BENGAL 17th Oct 1793.

DEAR BRETHREN.

Twice before this time have I written in expectation of an Opportunity to send to you—but was disappointed, once was in the Bay of Biscay, by the Frigate which convoyed us out, but when she parted with us the sea run too high to send out a boat—and again we expected to put in at the Cape of Good Hope, but as there was a prospect of arriving at Bengal, before the Change of the Monsoon we did not put in there, or any where else; thus far through the mercy of God, however we are safe arrived, and all in good health; thinking that we shall be pretty much engaged after our arrival, I begin my letters here.

The whole of our stay in England is known to you, and all that befel us there, we waited at Dover till Thursday Morning the 13th June. when we were called up, and saw the ship lying off the Harbour, about five oclock, we came on board, where we met with the greatest civility—which has continued till this day— the ship is called Kron Princess Marie, commanded by Capt J. Christmas an Englishman, whose own is the ship and Cargo;—and who is one of the most polite, accomplished Gentlemen, who ever sustained the name of a Sea Captain—He immediately ordered the great Cabin to be separated, that we might be well accomo- dated—so that we have a large cabin half the width of the ship with Sash Windows & the sides papered be- sides a smaller one—Mr Thomas likewise has a cabin, and tho' we went for so small a sum (all the other passengers having paid 100 guineas each) yet no kind of distinction has been observed, but we have all met with the same kind treatment.—Four more Passengers are with us in the ship, two of them English, and two of them French men—One of the French men is the most presumptuous hardened Deist that I ever saw or

heard of; I have almost every day been engaged in
Disputes with him, but to no purpose his dernier ressort is to turn all into Badinage—his credit however
has sunk very much in the ship upon that very
account—The Captain is a man of very extensive reading but never meddles with anything that is written
upon Religion. He is *half brother* to *Lady Langham of
Cottesbrooke* the men are Danes & Norway men and
if there is no religion among them yet there is much
less irreligion and Prophaness than among the English. Our first mate is son of the *Superintendent* of a
district of Norway and from all that I can learn there
is more real Godliness among the Established Lutherans of those countries than in the English Establishment. They seem to be more upon a level with the
Scots—but toleration is more extensive there than in
England for no civil Penalties or disabilities are im-
posed upon any people for Religion.

Our voyage has been on the whole very agreeable
and pleasant tho' we have had some rough weather,
and have experienced many great deliverances. June
the 13 Sailed from Dover. 15th in the Bay of Biscay
24 fell in with the Trade wind, 25 passed the Island
of Madeira, 27th passed Palma one of the Canaries and
saw Gomara and Fera, but could not get a sight of
Teneriff. Saw Flying fish—29 passed the Tropic of
Cancer—the heat by the Thermometer 72° July 2. Be-
calmed between the Cape Verd Islands and Africa heat

86° 21st passed the line Augt 1st passed the Tropic of Capricorn and on the 20th were off the Cape of Good Hope, Our Course was by the Islands of Trinidada, Saxenburg, Tristham de Cunhas and then from Lat 27 S Long 29 W straight to the cape, hitherto our voyage had been very prosperous and nothing of a distressing Nature had happened, but in the morning of the 26th we had a very distressing accident—[There is a bank, extends, into the sea from Cape des Aquitas, the most southern part of Africa for about eighty Leagues South—upon which runs a strong current and which when it meets the wind raises the sea in a very tremendous manner—We were in S. Lat 38° and thought ourselves secure from that Danger, but about one in the morning I was awakened by the violent rolling of the ship—and found stools tables &c rolling about the Cabin—and presently Pots, Glasses & everything in the ship which was not secured were Crashing at once.

I arose and put all to rights in our Cabin, was just got into bed again when Mr Thomas came to the Door, and told me that we had carried away our Fore, and Main Topmasts; I begged my wife & children to keep in bed for fear of having their bones broken and went upon Deck—where the scene was shocking indeed—The night (tho' very providentially the moon shone) the Sea like Mountains beating the Ship in all directions, the masts, yards, Sails & Rigging hanging over the sides and Beating against the ship, and the men upon them, in every part to unrig them and let them loose, all on board have uniformly declared that they never saw anything like it, and one time we concluded that she was going to the bottom—Our ship is about 130 feet long in the Keel, her Burden about 600 Tons—she was mounted on the top of a sea which could not be less than 50 or 60 yards in height from which she decended head foremost almost perpendicularly, or quite as near it as the roof of an House :—I saw her going—and concluded with others that she could not recover it, had but a moment to Reflect, felt resigned to the Will of God—and to prevent being tossed overboard by the motion caught hold of what was nearest to me—the plunge was dreadful ; her Bowsprit was under water—and the Jibboom which is fastened to the Bow Sprit carried away—but in a moment she recovered the Plunge, and mounted upon another Sea, without shipping an Hogshead of water—at last we cleared the wreck, and set our main sail which kept the ship a little Steady—in four days after this we had a violent gale ; but except the uncomfortable rolling of the ship we sustained no damage—it took us up eleven days to repair our loss—] and only two days after that, a violent squall carried away our new Main Topmast Our fore topmast was weak, and could not bear a Gallant mast, so that we were forced to put up a Jury mast for the main Topmast, and as the ship was victualled for only four months, and we had but little water left, the Captain determined to go into Mauritius, to refit— but strong Northerly Winds prevented our going that way. With care we came this place the rains have supplied us with plenty of water—And except a black woman and child who were very ill when they came on board and died off the Cape of Good Hope, and the Carpenter, who, by the very great exertions which he was obliged to make on account of our misfortunes, caught cold, which was succeeded by a pleurisy and followed by the scurvy of which he died when we were within six day sail of Bengal—we have had good health—our infant has thrived more than if it had been on land, and the children are as well satisfied.

We have not been entirely destitute of Religious opportunities. Family worship has been constantly attended to, and every Lord's day we have had preaching twice in our cabin. Our congregation has sometimes consisted of six persons besides our own family— they consisted of Norway & Holstein men, Danes, English, Flemings, & French, or rather one of each ; with respect to religious persuasion they were Lutherans Papists and Calvinists—we had some very pleasant seasons, but have been of no use that I know of. Many private seasons I have enjoyed of great pleasure, and have a growing satisfaction in having undertaken this work ; and a growing desire for its success ; though I feel so much barrennesss, and so little of

3

that lively continual sense of divine things upon
my mind that I almost despair of ever being of any
Use ; but in General I feel a pleasure in the thought
that Christ has promised to be with his Ministers to
the end of the World, and that as our Day is, so shall
our strength be.   I have often felt much pleasure in
recollecting the times of Publick worship in the
Churches in England, and reflecting that, now perhaps,
Hundreds, if not Thousands are praying for me ; you
will also easily believe, that my Friends have not been
forgotten by me on these occasions.—Your 10 oClock
in the morning will be our 4 in the afternoon, there
being 6 Hours difference of time between you & us.
Mr Thomas has laboured indefatiguably in translating
the Book of Genesis which he has now accomplished,
in short we are now expecting to join Ram Boshee,
& Parbotee in a few days.]

I hope the Society will go on and increase and that
the multitudes of Heathen in the World may hear the
Glorious words of Truth—Africa is but a little way
from England—Madagascar but a little further, South
America, and all the Numerous and Large Islands in
the Indian & Chinese Seas, I hope will not be passed
over, a large field opens on every side and millions of
perishing Heathens tormented in this life by means of
Idolatry, Superstition, and Ignorance, and subject to
eternal Misery in the next, are pleading, Yes all, their
miseries plead, as soon as they are known, with every

Heart that loves God ; and with all the Churches of
the living God ;—O that many labourers may be thrust
out into the Vineyard of our Lord Jesus Christ—and
that the Gentiles may come to the Knowledge of the
Truth as it is in him. You will do us very great service if you send us out a Polyglot Bible, (there is one
at Collis's) by the next conveyance ; Ram Boshee is a
good Persian Scholar, and it will certainly help us much,
if you can get a copy of the Gospels *in Malay* it will be
an help to us, and I wish you to send me all that are
published of *Curtis's Botanical Magazine* and *Sowerby's
English Botany* from No 77 of Curtis and No 31 of
Sowerby—and to continue sending them regularly, and
deduct what they cost from my allowance. Whatsoever
is published of note in England, especially among the
Baptists I hope you will be sure to send and I hope
that in return we may be able to send to you tidings
that will rejoice your hearts.

Nov 16th. After beating about and being driven
back by currents for near a Month we arrived in Bala-
sore Roads on the 7th inst and on the 10th Mr T and
I began our labours—we came in a Ponvowah from the
ship—and at slack water we lay to—at a Bouar or
Market—where Mr T preached to the people they
left their merchandise immediately and listened for
three hours with great attention—one of them prepared us a dinner—which we eat—a Plaintain leaf was
our Dish & Plates—and instead of Knives & forks we

used our fingers—when we left them, they desired us
to come again—Poor Ram Boshee was waiting for us
but to our great grief he has been bowing down to
Idols again—he was forsaken by European Christians
and discarded by *Hindoos*—and he says I was very
ill of a Flux—nothing to support me or my family—
All said Mr T would never return—I knew that
Roman Catholics worshipped Idols. I thought I had
seen but a small part of the Bible, perhaps the worship of images might be commanded in some part of
it which I had not seen, I hesitated, and I complied
but it was for a piece of bread, but I still love Christianity much the best.

25. Ram Boshee still keeps close to us, I have
engaged him now as my Moonshee—and am often
much pleased with his conversation, we also hear that
Parbotee stands well, and that he and Mohem Chune
are coming down to us—we are today making ap-
plication to the Governor for uncultivated Lands to
settle upon which (if we can obtain them) will be an
asylum for those who lose cast for the Gospels sake.—
I have had several conversations with a Brahman who
speaks English well—and being unable to defend himself against the Gospel, He intends to come attended by
a *Pundit* and try the utmost of their strength.—having
so many letters to write I must leave off—We are
all well—the climate at this (which is the Cold Season)
is not disagreeable, except it be the great difference

between the Heat of Day & night—which is often 10 Degrees—but the heat is quite tolerable— Mr T will give an account of proper articles of Trade to send out, and as our Families are so different, and I have the expence of a Moonshee too—I hope the Society will settle the proportion between us—The more I know the more I love him—He is a very holy man —but his faithfulness often degenerates into Personality (tho' not to me for we live in the greatest Love) which may account for the difference between Mr Grant & him. My family is well, all Join in love to you, your people ; all ministers, and Christians that you see & write to, & the Society especially

I am Yours most affectly.

W CAREY

MR FULLER

Dec. 16th.

Since writing the above, we have been near a month at Bandel a Portugese settlement, we have given up our intentions of applying for Waste Lands at Present, on account of the Danger from the Tigers, and the expense of Cultivation—but we are now going further up the country perhaps to *Nuddea*, *Cutiva*, *Gowr*, or *Maloa*, but as it is uncertain which—I must wish you to direct all Letters to either Mr T or me—to be left at the Post Office Calcutta till called for.

We have frequent Opportunities of addressing the Hindoos, and their attention is astonishing—last Lord's

day we went, and Mr Thomas preached to near two
Hundreds of them at Saa-Gunge a village near us—
they listened with great Seriousness, and several followed us to make further enquiries about what is the
way to Heaven, and how they should do to walk therein
—every place presents a pleasing prospect to us of success—and we are of one mind and one soul—pray for
us—we duly remember you—and the prosperity of the
Society lies very near our Hearts

W CAREY

Rev A. FULLER
                Kettering
                    Northamptonshire

There is a peculiar interest attaching to this letter to
those who read it in the light of the events that have
succeeded its writing, and it is not difficult for the
imagination to picture the varying emotions with
which it must have been received by the friends of
Carey in England, and by those who, far from being
his friends, had looked upon his embassy as the wildest
and most dangerous of chimeras. To the hostile critic
there was not a little in the letter to furnish material
for jest and ridicule. The quaint phraseology, the
almost child-like expressions of wonder at the new
sights and terrors of the sea, the exaggerated estimates
of the immensity of waves fifty or sixty yards high,
were easy subjects for the perverted ingenuity of the
satirist, and it is scarcely remarkable that these letters

and the similar ones that followed should have seemed to men like Sydney Smith only the vaporings of igno-rant and diseased zeal. But to those who had, like Andrew Fuller, come to know more of the deep pur-pose that dominated the life of William Carey and of that passion for souls which mastered all his activity, the apparent crudities must have vanished away, and the only feeling that could have been left in the mind must have been one of profound admiration for the man who, without stopping to count the cost, and with scarcely any intelligent apprehension of the perils and dangers that he had to incur, had flung himself reso-lutely into the vanguard of what all but he and a few like-minded associates must have regarded as the most forlorn of hopes. But to-day, as we read the narrative, when a century has gone by, and the writer and his critics have all passed, leaving words only to be their judges, there can be little doubt as to what the verdict of history shall be, and the most merciful judgment that will be likely to be passed upon the critic will be that of Carey on poor Ram Boshee—that he knew no better.

The letter that follows owes its chief interest to the fact that it was written from Debarta, where, for a little time, the missionaries hoped they might find the oppor-tunity of establishing a station within the Company's territory. But events proved that the judgment of the natives, as Carey records it, that " Englishmen are worse than 'Tygers'' was not altogether out of the way, for it was Englishmen and not tigers who drove the little missionary colony from English territory to seek a harbor on Danish soil ; and the next letter which we present to the reader, signed by all of the five missionaries, and dated at Serampore April 25, 1800, gives the account of the formation of the first Baptist Church in India, and of the foundation of the first permanent mission undertaken by the Society to the Hindoos.

DEBARTA *Feby* 15th, 1794.

MY DEAR FRIEND

I do not expect that you will receive this till some time after the other letters, the last ships being hastened away upon account of the numerous Privateers fitted out from *Mauritius*. On this account also I shall not be able to write to so many of my friends in England as I wished, being even uncertain whether even this will arrive at Calcutta soon enough for the ships.— Nor have I anything of importance to communicate more than I have already written—except that Mr T is now settled in his profession at Calcutta—where he pursues the Mission also, and I have taken a few acres of Land at *Hasuabad* near this place; which is about 40 miles East of Calcutta upon the River *Juboua*—I am now at the house of a *Mr Short*, a Servant of the Company, who generously invited us all, tho' before entirely unknown to him, to stay at his house till we have erected one of our own; and which I am now engaged in. The Walls will be made with mats fastened to Posts of Wood, and the roof with Bamboo and Thatched; In this work the neighbouring inhabitants yield me a little assistance, and a great number of people, about four or five hundred families intend to come and reside in our neighbourhood, this is principally occasioned by Moonshee telling them that I am not like the other Englishmen, but that I shall be like a Father to them, the Country is an excellent soil, but has lately been deserted almost upon account of the Tygers, and other Beasts of prey which infest the Place; but all these are afraid of a Gun, and will be soon expelled—this people therefore are not afraid when an European is nigh—but have kept from other's because they think Englishmen worse than Tygers; We shall have all the nesscessaries of Life except Bread for which rice must be a substitute—Wild hogs, Deers & Fowls are to be procured by the Gun & must supply us with a considerable part of our food, and in the woods'—there are Rhinoceros's which are good food, but is dangerous going after them for fear of Tygers— the greatest inconvenience I find is that of our being separated so far, and having so much of my time necessarily taken up in procuring provisions, and cultivating my little Farm. When my House is built however I shall have much more leisure, than I now have, and shall have daily opportunity of conversing with the

natives and pursuing the work of the Mission ;   There
is certainly a large field here for usefulness, much
larger than you conceive, both amongst the Hindoos,
and Mussulmen.   They are very numerous very in-
quisitive, and very attentive to the Gospel ; when I can
so far know the Language as to preach in it, I have no
doubt of having a stated Congregation ; and I much
hope to send you some more pleasing accounts than at
present I can.   I can so far converse in the Language
as to be understood in most things belonging to Eating
& Drinking, Buying, and Selling &ct and my ear is
somewhat familiarised to the Bengalic Sounds.

It is a language of a very singular Construction
having no Plurals except to Pronouns ; and not a
singular Preposition in it—but the Cases of Nouns and
Pronouns are almost endless, all the words answering
to our prepositions, being put after the word and forming a new *Case ;* Excepting these irregularities I find
it an easy Language.

I never felt myself more happy in any undertaking
than this and tho' I never felt the loss of Social Religion so much as now yet a consciousness of having
given up all for God, is a support and the work with
all its attendant inconveniences is to me a rich reward.

I hope the Society still prospers and think they would
do well if they would still keep their eye towards
Africa or Asia—these countries are not like the wilds
of America where long labour will scarce collect sixty

people to hear the word, for here it is almost impossible to go out of the way of Hundreds and Preachers are wanted a thousand times more than people to preach to, there are in India the Mahrattas Country, and all the Northern parts to Cashmere, and not a soul that thinks of God aright. I have been mentioned to Government, by a person high in office, and utterly unknown to, and unthought of by me, as a proper person to send to Tibet, and Assam, to make discoveries which they have much at Heart. Should this take place, it would open a new and wide door for usefulness in a Country, remote from the Knowledge of European's; but at present many obstacles are in the way, all these nations are afraid that the English have designs to subjugate them as they have Bengal——however there is work enough here or any where else in this Country.

My wife & two Children have been very ill indeed of the Bloody Flux I believe occasioned by the Cold nights, succeeding to Hot Days. The Thermometer differing about 15 or 20 degrees between day & night—but they are mercifully recovered.

I hope you will send me an account of every thing Important in the Churches,—especially Leicester,—my love to all Ministers—all Christians, your own people, &c. [especially remember me to Mrs Wallis, Mr Gotch —Timms, Hobson, &ct for I dont know where to stop —Inform Mr Hogg, that it is impossible to send him the small Quantity of Sugar he mentioned to me without   it which neither himself or me could approve of.   I have enclosed the wings of a Flying fish which flew on board our ship, they may be acceptable as a Curiosity]

You must not expect my Journal till next year.   I regularly keep one which I intend then to Transmit. [My particular love to Messrs Ryland, Sutcliff & Morris

I am yours very affectly.

WM CAREY

[Direct to me or Mr T at Calcutta to be Left at the Post Office]

Revd. A FULLER

Kettering

Northamptonshire

SORAMPOOR

25th *April* 1800

DEARLY BELOVED BRETHREN

Scarce any thing gives us more pleasure than thus to write to you, except it be the reception of letters from you.   Letters which (some of us at least can say) have often rejoiced our hearts ; not merely as expressions of *your* regard for *Us*, but as conveying to us the pleasing Intelligence of the Growing Interest of our LORD in those parts of the world which you are more conversant with than ourselves.

We have agreed to write *four* Public Letters (at least) every year ; to be drawn up by each Brother in Rotation and signed by the Whole. [The last was written the latter end of February or beginning of March. From that time to the Present we have dwelt in the Midst of noise ; the sound of Axes & Hammers.

But now our Business of this kind is drawing to a close : The House & Premises we thought good to purchase, were well worth the price we paid for them. But to accomodate them to so large a Family, or rather to so many Families as we consist of, has occasioned considerable labour & expense. We have built a schoolhouse—a Verandah on the South side of the Dwelling House in order to break off the violence of the Sun, and to serve as a lodging room for the Scholars we hope to have. Besides these a long train of Expenses have occurred in paper for Printing &c &c. We have already drawn on you for £829 "11 "6 in the manner following.—)

						£
In favour	of Captain Passmore	.	.	600
Do	"	" Mr Dexter	.	.	.	25
Do	"	" Mr Dickson	.	.	.	172–4–6
Do	"	" Mr Powell	.	.	.	7–7–
Do	"	" Mr Dalton	.	.	.	25

£829 " 11 " 6

This Sum is all expended : Nor is it in our power to Negociate any more Bills at present. A kind friend however has just lent us 1000 Rupees at 6 per cent in half the Coys Interest.

You will please therefore to send us Relief as soon as possible. Send as much money as you can, not only that our Wants may be relieved, but that we may put it out to interest. On the first of May the school will be opened from wch we hope to derive considerable assistance and so lighten your Burdens. We cannot indeed tell how it may succeed, but from the kindness of friends, we have much reason to hope that it will prosper]

Though we have had much business upon our *Hands* since we have been at this place, our Hearts have not been taken from the one grand Object.

We have gone on Translating & revising the Scriptures—Preaching the Word—and Learning the Language. Brother Ward assisted by Brother Brunsdon has been busily employed in Printing Hymns & Copies of the Commandments. They are now printing a Book for the use of Schools, compiled by Bror *Marshman ;* intended more immediately for our own school, but which we hope will be acceptable in others. Upon examining the Bengalle Types it is found that a few Pholas are wanting. These we hope to have complete in a week or ten day's from this time, and then to begin printing the Holy Shastro of our God, which in due time shall bring Human ones into contempt. We find now that we must not only *Print* Books but *Bind* them also. We cannot deliver the Bible out in an unbound state, nor indeed anything else that we may ever Publish.

Besides we have many books amongst us ruining for the want of Binding— This business we intend to have done in our own House, for wch you will please to send the articles mentioned in the inclosed Paper. We trust Brethren, that we have great reason to Bless our GOD for bringing us to Serampoor. The attention that has been paid to us, seems to be a token for Good, that the LORD will establish us, and make us useful. We have Public Preaching in English every Lord's Day morning, wch is attended by the Governor and many other Europeans in the Place. Brethren *Carey* & *Fountain* preach also morning & evening in the streets of Serampoor & the adjacent villages. Brahmins have been put to shame while other Casts have heard the word with attention. Many come to dispute with Bror Carey. Some for Instruction—others to enquire the time of worship. A Free school is building for the natives, which has given pleasure to most who have heard thereof.

As a family we live together in peace, and increase in Love to one another. The Lord has been good to each of us in preserving our Health. Dear Sister Brunsdon gets stout & well. The children are all remarkably healthy. The small pox being very prevalent at Calcutta, we have had them Innoculated, and they have now recovered therefrom. They had it so lightly as scarce to make them ill. In consequence of all the goodness we have experienced. and the pleasing prospects before us, we consecrated yesterday as a day of *Thanksgiving*. as also to the taking into the Church the Brethren & Sisters lately arrived. The business of the Day was conducted in the following Manner.—

Met at 6 oclock in the morning, when Bror Ward began by reading the 23rd and 103rd Psalms, after wch he read out a hymn and Prayed. All the Brethren followed in the same excercises. This meeting lasted two hours—Met again at 10/oclock, Bror Fountain began by reading 1st Timothy 3rd. Singing & Prayer. After this the Dismissions of the Brethren & Sisters from their respective Churches were read by Bror Carey, and the Right Hand of Fellowship given to each by him & Bror Fountain as a token of acceptance.

Agreed that Sister Brunsdon (having left England before she had an opportunity of procuring her Dismission from Lairford Church) have Communion with us at the LORD's table till her Dismission arrives.

Agreed that Bror Carey be the Pastor of this Church & Brethren Fountain and Marshman the two Deacons.

Agreed that the Ordinance of the Lords Supper be Administered to us the first Sabbath in every Kalendar Month.—After this business the Brethren related the manner in which they were brought to the Knowledge of the Truth.

Bror Carey concluded in prayer. Met again at 4/ oclock P.M. Brother Marshman read the " Address of the Committee of the Baptist Society " delivered May. 7. 1799.—A Letter from Bror Pearce of Birmingham— And an address by Brother Booth of London.

May the LORD impress their sentiments on our Minds. Bror Carey concluded in prayer.—During this meeting the following Address was voted to the Governor of the Settlement.

" To the Honourable Colonel BIE.

" SIR.

" Having set apart this day in our family to return thanks to GOD for the establishment of our Missionary Settlement in this country, we could not but recollect the many gracious, and important favours which we have received at your hands. We have prayed, and shall not cease to pray that our Heavenly father may pour his most sacred Benediction upon you, and long make you a blessing to the World. We hope our Conduct will always show that our Gratitude is sincere and that we aim at being truly the Disciples, of him who exhibited a perfect pattern of Universal obedience.

4

" Accept, Sir, our fervent, and united Acknowledgments ; in which we know our Society in England would be very happy to concur.

We are, Sir,

Your most affectionate &

obedient Servants

WM. CAREY

WM. WARD

JOHN FOUNTAIN

DANL. BRUNSDON

JOSHUA MARSHMAN "

Met again at 8 oClock in the evening for more Public worship. Bror Forsyth, a Paedo Baptist missionary (whom we had previous invited) engaged in Prayer. Brother Carey afterwards preached an Animating sermon from Romans 12. ver 12th "Rejoicing in Hope."

This morning the above address was presented to the Governor. He was considerably affected by it, and assured the Brethren who waited upon him, that it gave him great pleasure to have us in the Settlement.

He has again and again declared that he would do every thing in his power to promote our Welfare. We hope the Society will never forget in their Prayers, the Man who shows so much kindness to us.

Were you also to vote him an Address of thanks it would be well received.

Yesterday's pleasure was considerably heightened

by the Arrival of English Letters for Bretheren Carey, Ward, & Brunsdon. We did not forget you in our prayers, nor could we refrain from Blessing God for your great and constant care of us. The Zeal & Generosity of our Scotch Brethren is surely beyond example! Pray let our United Thanks be presented to them. One circumstance however was a matter of grief to us vizt. The Capture of the Ship Duff. We will not cease to pray for the dear Missionaries on Board her, that the Lord their God may prosper them wherever they go. This is our Joint prayer—May the Kingdom of our LORD come with Power.

We are Dear Brethren

in endless affection

Yours

WM. CAREY

J. FOUNTAIN

J. MARSHMAN

W. WARD

D. BRUNSDON.

The two letters here given, with the preceding one, furnish a brief epitome of the history of the Mission up to the time when the correspondence began which it is the chief purpose of this little book to set forth. But before proceeding to introduce that correspondence, it may be well to give a hasty sketch of the man who was largely instrumental in bringing the new missionary movement into prominence in the American churches; and to do this, it is necessary to go back again to a little English hamlet less known even than the quiet town of Olney.

On the somewhat barren and rocky slopes of the range of hills whose loftiest summit is the peak of Snowdon, in North Wales, nestles the little village of Y Garn, and near that hamlet lies the farm known for generations as Plas Llecheiddior. Exactly when the old farm-house was built no one seems to know, and speculation is still rife as to the meaning of the name. Some have suggested that it signifies the " Place of the Ivied Rock"; others, that it simply means " Pleasant Place"; but family tradition has it that the true meaning is, " The place where Ior hid himself"; and till recent years a rude niche was pointed out in the wall of the stone farm-house, where the fabled Ior was said to have taken refuge in some dire local disturbance. At this old farm-house, which had for some hundred and fifty years been in the possession of his forefathers as peasant farmers, there was born on the 8th of March, 1767, John Williams, a sturdy Welsh lad, but with a lameness from birth which unfitted him for the agricultural pursuits of his father and kinsfolk. It was his father's desire that he should prepare himself to enter the ministry of the Established Church; but not finding himself in sympathy with that Church, he at first determined to acquire a trade, and, for that purpose, took up his residence in the not distant town of Carnarvon. Having, however, become converted at about the age of nineteen, he determined to study for the ministry, and a few years later, leaving the Independent Church, with which he had first united, he was immersed, and became a member of the Horeb Baptist Church at Garn. Shortly after this he was called to the pastorate of that Church, and remained their pastor for some years. But in the summer of 1795, he determined to leave Wales and take up his residence in the United States, a resolution which he carried into effect, reaching New York July 25th. Within a fortnight after his arrival, his younger brother, who had accompanied him, suddenly died, and Mr. Williams himself was prostrated by illness. The history of the days that followed, and of the settlement of Mr. Williams as pastor of the Fayette Street Baptist Church, is best given in the language of his gifted son and successor in the ministry, Rev. William R. Williams, D.D., who was his biographer. As the biography has, however, long been out of print, a short extract from it will not be out of place :

" He had left his native soil, his family, and his friends, to find in a foreign land, and among a people of strange language, a grave for the companion of his voyage, a beloved brother. He began to doubt if he had not rashly ventured where God had not called him ; and this consideration seemed to raise his feelings, which were naturally acute, to a pitch of intense agony. It was but the prelude and the promise of after usefulness ; it was in a manner the parting blow of the adversary—the struggle in and by which, his heavenly Father was girding and exercising him for his appointed task. In his distress he prayed that one, though but one, soul might be granted to him in America as the fruit of his ministry and the proof of his calling ; and when he arose from the bed of sickness, he arose, if possible, more anxiously earnest than ever, in the work of his heart. He had intended to have settled in some neighborhood inhabited by Welsh emigrants, and in his mother language to have continued his ministerial labours ; and with this view, his attention had been directed to Beulah, in Pennsylvania, and Steuben, in New York. In Welsh he delivered his first sermon in America. It was preached in the meeting-house then occupied by the Rev. John Stanford, in Fair Street.

"The Baptist church in Oliver (at that time Fayette) Street, was then composed of about thirty members, of whom, however, only twenty could be found, who met in a small unfinished wooden building, about thirty feet square, without galleries, and seated with benches instead of pews. This church permitted him and his countrymen occasionally to use their place of worship for service in their own language. They also encouraged Mr. W. to attempt the acquisition of the English language, a request with which, after some hesitation, he complied, and began to preach in English for one part of the Sabbath, on the other part still continuing the use of the Welsh. Through every disadvantage, the English brethren saw a deep and fervent piety, and a native vigour of mind, which greatly delighted them. They had made several attempts to procure a supply, but were unable to find one in all respects suitable. They now began to fix their hopes upon the young stranger, and at length, after a trial of nine months, Mr. Williams became, on their unanimous request, their pastor on the 28th of August, 1798. In the summer of this year, the yellow fever commenced one of its most dreadful attacks upon the city of New York. Mr. W., among others, was early seized with the contagion, and his life was despaired of. But the decisive conduct of his physician proved, under God, the means of his recovery, and he again appeared with new zeal among the people of his charge. Encouraged by the attention which he excited, in January following the little church substituted pews for benches. But they grew, and the place soon became too strait, and in 1800, the meeting-house was enlarged to sixty by forty-three feet, and galleries were added. In the course of years this place also became insufficient; and in little more than twenty years after his first settlement, Mr. W. saw raised the third meeting-house, the present edifice, a large stone building, sixty-four by ninety-four feet.''

The building referred to as having been erected in 1800 is that shown in the accompanying sketch, taken from an old print in *Valentine's Manual*, the only source now available for a view of the old church. It was here that John Williams labored; and in his ministry in the city he came into contact with many other representatives of various Christian denominations, in whose work he took an interest second only to that he felt for the work among his own people.

The New York Missionary Society, an inter-denominational Society, seems to have been formed at least as early as 1796, and from the earliest list of its officers now to be found (those for 1799), it would appear that Dr. John Rodgers was President, and the Rev. John M. Mason, the friend of Alexander Hamilton, was the Secretary. With the work of this Society Mr. Williams seems to have made himself early familiar, and in the report of the Society at the annual meeting in April, 1801, Mr. Williams' name appears on the list of Directors. To this report there is appended a letter signed by William Carey and dated Serampore, October 15, 1800. It is, of course, impossible to say at this date through what channel this letter was forwarded to the New York Missionary Society; but it seems natural to

BAPTIST CHURCH IN FAYETTE STREET, NEW YORK.

conjecture that it was forwarded along with the letter next placed before the reader and addressed to John Williams by Dr. Carey in the year 1800. Before setting out this letter, however, it may be well to allude to the work which had been done by the New York Missionary Society. As already stated, this Society was inter-denominational, and seems to have directed most of its attention to mission work among the North American Indians. This work had been, it would appear, largely carried on among the Chickasaw Indians, but it soon became evident to the Directors of the Association that other work might be done, and how the work came to be done will, perhaps, best be shown by a short extract from the report of the Directors already referred to, in 1801 :

" Their first undertaking having been thus far countenanced by the Lord of the harvest, and their resources being by no means exhausted, the Directors felt it their duty to turn their eyes to some other quarter which might invite a new mission. An event, which they cannot but account providential, pointed out the North-Western Indians, especially the Tuscarora and Seneca nations, as the most proper objects of their next attempt. The New York Baptist Association, who were already known to some Indian tribes, wishing to carry still farther among them the light of the knowledge of the glory of God in the face of Jesus Christ, but desti-

tute of the requisite means, recommended the Rev.
Elkanah Holmes, one of their number, as a suitable
Missionary.   In this gentleman, who had formerly ex-
perience of similar service, the Directors found those
solid, evangelical principles, that zeal for the salvation
of the Heathen, that natural sagacity and disposition
for enterprise, and that acquaintance with Indian character and custom, which rendered him peculiarly fit
for the contemplated mission.   They accordingly took
him into the employment of the Society, and having
furnished him with special instructions, set him apart
to his work by solemn prayer.

" This Mission being designed, both by Mr. Holmes,
and the Directors, rather as a Mission of experiment,
than a permanent establishment, he was employed for
six months ; but not so limited by his appointment as
to prevent his spending a longer time in making ex-
cursions of inquiry among the remoter tribes.   For his
compensation, while engaged in this labour of love, the
Directors have voted a salary at the rate of 375 dollars
per annum, beside his travelling expenses.

" All the accounts which have been received from him
and of him, are singularly gratifying.   The Brotherton
and New-Stockbridge Indians, contributed their assistance with a promptness and fervour truly Christian.
Their addresses to Mr. Holmes breathe a spirit which
ought to shame the languor, and quicken the efforts
of those who have enjoyed superior privileges."

This extract explains the allusion in the letters that follow to the Rev. Elkanah Holmes and his work among the Indians ; and it was probably some allusion to the work of the New York Missionary Society which induced Dr. Carey to send to Mr. Williams with his letter a copy of the Gospel by Matthew for presentation to this Society. However that may be, one thing is certain, that either in the early part of the year 1800 or, possibly, in the closing months of the preceding year, John Williams addressed a letter to William Carey giving some account of the work of the New York Missionary Society among the North American Indians, and invited correspondence as to the work that Dr. Carey was doing in India. In reply to this letter Carey penned the following :

MY DEAR BROTHER.

The Honour you have done me in writing to me in connection with Brethren Thomas and Fountain induces me to write to you.

I can also assure you that it is with great pleasure I embrace the opportunity of corresponding with the friends of our Lord Jesus in your distant part of the World. One of our Brethren viz, Brother Fountain, was removed from us to the church above on the 20th August last ; his affliction (a dysentery) was very painful, but his hope was full of immortality and his death bore a testimony to the truth of the Gospel which was very encouraging to the spectators and left a sweet savour of the excellence of Gospel truth.

In the last year our Number was augmented by the coming of four new Missionaries from England ; they came in the American ship " Criterion " of Philadelphia commanded by that excellent man Capt. B. Wickes a man whose name is always spoken of with the utmost respect by all our Brethren, and whose piety was admired by them all.   You will be informed from England I expect, before this reaches you, that Brother Grant died very soon after his arrival ; the others, viz, Brethren Marshman, Ward and Brunsdon with myself and our wives and children form a common Family, and live in the utmost harmony ; we love one another and are as the heart of one man in our Work.   Our habitation is now at Serampore, a Danish settlement about 14 Miles from Calcutta, at which place we have purchased a House for the Mission, and enjoy the protection of that Government.   The situation which I was in before, viz, Mudnabutty was near 400 Miles north of this place.   I trust our going there as it appeared absolutely necessary at the time we went has not been altogether in vain.   We could not have lived there longer, or if we had could not have carried on our operations with the freedom we now can, and it is highly probable that we should not have been suffered to work our printing press in so distant a part of the company's dominions, though we should have said nothing about politics, it being our constant rule to keep clear of that rock.

We have a press and types for the Bengalee language and are printing the Bible. We began first with the New Testament and have finished the four Gospels and begun to compose the Acts of the Apostles, several small tracts, poems, hymns, etc. have also been printed in that language and dispersed. This part of the country is very populous and as full of idolatry as it can hold. Capt. Hague will inform you of this from what he has seen. He was here, and went out with us one evening when we went out to preach to the heathen. I suppose that no people can have more completely surrendered their reason than the Hindoos. In all matters of business and every thing relating to this world, they are not deficient in knowledge, but in all things relating to religion, they are apparently void of all understanding. Their books abound with the most abominable stories, and the characters of their gods are drawn in colour so black that even the father of wickedness himself would scarcely own. The Hindoos are not fond of hearing in detail the vices of their gods, yet so devoted are they to their old customs, that they constantly adore characters the most detestable. It is not to be thought that the moral character of a people should be better than that of their gods. Men made themselves idols *after their own hearts*, and therefore to look for good morals among idolaters is the height of folly. The conduct of the Hindoos but too fully proves the truth of this observation, for they are literally sunk into the dregs of vice. 'T is true they have not the savage ferocity of American Indians but this is abundantly supplied with a dreadful stock of *low cunning* and deceit. Moral rectitude makes no part of their religious system, therefore, no wonder that they are sunk, nay wholly immersed in all manner of impurity.

Within a few months past the gospel of Matthew and other small pieces have been circulated among them, this is the introduction of a thing, a light entirely new, and has evidently awakened the fears of many of the Brahmans. Public disputes with them also in the streets, and any place where we meet with them and always in the hearing of the common people have in some measure excited them to reflect, but at present it has been of no use except to make them try to avoid disputes with us and to excite a laugh against them among others who are not permitted to read for themselves. I have no doubt but in the end the God of all grace will exert His almighty power and vindicate His authority and establish the glory of His own name in this wretched country ; our labors may be only like those of pioneers to prepare the way, but truth will assuredly prevail and this among the other kingdoms of the earth shall assuredly see the salvation of our God. I doubt not but a few more years will show Brahmans renouncing their cast, believing in Christ and throwing their idols to the moles and to the bats.

You can scarcely form an idea of the pleasure we all felt in receiving your letter and the very pleasing accounts of what our Lord is doing in your parts. We hope you will take every opportunity of dropping us a letter, and shall endeavor to reply to your correspondence at all times ; as to your letters finding us, the Captain who brings them has only to do as Captain Hague has done, send a man on purpose or come himself or on receiving a note any of us would wait on him.

I wrote the above about two months ago, but did not close the letter because I thought something might transpire before the sailing of Captain Hague which I should be glad to communicate. The ship will sail in a few days, I therefore close this by informing you that I have reason to hope the Lord has been working among the Hindoos ; one has given himself to the church, and we hope to baptize him in a very few days. Four more, viz. two men and two women appear truly wrought upon and give us hope that this is the first fruit of an approaching harvest. I hoped that Captain Hague might have been a spectator of their baptism, but he will go before it can take place. I, however, hope to be able to send an account of it to Dr. Rogers of Philadelphia, who has favored us with his correspondence and I trust you will hear the news from him.   The Philadelphia ship will not sail till a month or two later.   Dear Brother, what shall I say more— pray for us and write to us by every opportunity, news from your distant part of the world will rejoice our hearts, above all inform us of the success of dear Mr. Holmes and any other missionaries among the heathen. Tell us the news of your churches and send any trifling publication.   We have received some intelligence from America of European concerns before we heard it from Europe.

We have sent two copies of the gospel by Matthew in Bengallee at the end of which are some other little tracts, hymns, etc., in that language, which we have dispersed, we beg your acceptance of one copy and also that you will present the other in our name to The New York Mission Society as a token of our sincere union with them in the great object of their undertaking.

I am, very affectionately yours,

WM. CAREY.

SERAMPORE, *Dec. 9th*, 1800.

It can scarcely be necessary to add many words of comment upon this most interesting of letters.   The very manner of its composition was such as to give it an intrinsic interest which few other letters in the whole correspondence could possess.   Written, most of it, before any direct result was manifest of the seven years of labor, it yet breathes no spirit of discontent or of despair, but gives a comprehensive view of the field and treats of the difficulties to be met and overcome with a wise foresight as far removed from hopelessness as it is from over-sanguine anticipation. Then comes a break in the narration ; for two months it is laid aside, and when the writer again takes up his pen, the Mission was no longer without a convert. Krishnu Pal, the first convert of modern Christian Missions in India, is the one referred to by Dr. Carey in the close of this letter. To the members of the Christian Church in England and America he is, perhaps, more generally known as the first native Evangelist, and the author of the familiar hymn translated by Dr. Marshman, and beginning with the lines :

> "O thou, my soul, forget no more
> The friend, who all thy miseries bore."

The correspondence thus commenced was actively carried on from that time, the next letters from Dr. Carey being dated respectively November 11, 1801, and June 15, 1802.

MY DEAR BROR.

An opportunity now offers for me to write you a few lines by my much esteemed friend Capt. Wickes of Philadelphia, and tho' I have but very little to say, yet I must say that little.

5

Since the separation of Capt. Hague from this place (by whom I wrote to you) we have been visited with the loss of two Missionaries by Death, viz : Bror Brunsdon, who died last July, and Bror Thomas, the first Missionary to this country, who died Oct. 13th last ; by these and the preceding deaths of Brethn Grant and Fountain, all in little more than two years, we are now reduced to three persons, who are men capable of action, and should be much discouraged had not our gracious Lord appeared for us in such a manner as to revive our hearts and encourage us amidst these scenes of Mortality.

The God who thus removed four of our Brethren in two years, has within the last year given us six from among the Heathen who have made an open profession of his Name by Baptism, and are now members of our Church, and also two others, one my eldest son, the other a gentleman born in China. These are added to our Church, besides whom we hope for some who are not joined to us * . . . gone to our Lord above, a woman who appears to have been savingly converted under a very heavy affliction of which she died, since that her husband has also been apprehended by Christ and gives us great pleasure. My second son and an-other young man also afford us very lively hopes, so that we glory in the midst of our afflictions.

The Lord has also provided in other things beyond

* Part of the letter torn away.

our utmost expectations, so that we are supplied with all things necessary for this Life; besides our school which has exceeded our hopes, providence has opened a way which was least expected of anything in the world. I was without any idea of such a thing ever taking place when I was chosen professor of the Bengalee and Sangskrit Languages in the College of Fort William; a circumstance of which I had no expectation till I was applied to by the Provost to know if I would accept it, and which with the advice of my brethren I did. I trust that I am not put into this situation without some especial end to be accomplished thereby. One benefit I already see, viz: a door opening for me to visit some of the native Portuguese who are Roman Catholics, but when afflicted I have found access to some of them, and hope the introduction may contribute to the eternal salvation of some of them, for they are indeed a people sitting in darkness and the Shadow of Death, as ignorant or perhaps more so than the Heathen, and universally despised by people of all ranks and descriptions.

I long to hear from you how do you do? How does the Work of God go on with you? I am glad to find that there are many revivals still in different parts of your highly favoured land. If Capt. Hague is in your neighborhood, give my love to him, and inform him of our circumstances; he will feel somewhat interested

therein.   Tell him when he comes to India again not
to forget his promise to me to furnish the Garden of
the Mission House with some American Productions.

Farewell, my dear Bror.   Pray for us that we may
be faithful to the end and that the word of the Lord in
our hands may be quick, and powerful, sharper than a
two edged sword, so that its glorious effects may be
seen in the destruction of Sin and Superstition and in
the erection of the Kingdom of our glorious Redeemer
in this Land of Darkness and the Shadow of Death.
My love to all who love the Lord Jesus Christ in sin-
cerity, I am

Very affecty Yours,

WM. CAREY.

COLLEGE OF FORT WILLIAM,
    Nov. 11, 1801.

DEAR BROTHER :—

I was very agreeably surprised by the arrival of
Captain Hague, and by the favor which he brought us
from yourself and other friends at New York.   Be
assured that I and my colleagues very highly esteem
your correspondence.

Blessed be the God and Father of our Lord Jesus
Christ, for the abundant mercy afforded by him to the
inhabitants of America.   Two thousand baptized in less
than a year !   I am astonished, I am filled with hope
and joy, my heart is enlarged, and I expect that very

soon the kingdoms of this world will become the kingdoms of our Lord and of his Christ ; and may it soon
be accomplished.

The prospect around us is very different. We are on
every side surrounded with heathens and Mahomme-
dans, who are deaf to the voice of reason, of Scripture,
and of God. This very day many thousands of people,
I suppose near a million, have met for the mean purpose of washing a piece of wood ; or, in other words, for
the purpose of bathing a wooden idol, near Serampore,
whose name is Juggernaut, which signifies " The Lord
of the World." Perhaps such a congregation never
met together to hear a gospel sermon since the world
began. This very idolatry, however, is probably sub-
servient to the spread of the gospel, for several who
came from a great distance and have only heard of us,
have come to beg a New Testament or some small
pamphlet, which we of course, are glad to give.

When we look around upon the multitudes who care
nothing about God, who are given up to every vice,
and to every lust, we are filled with distress, and sometimes yield for a season to discouragement ; and indeed it is a melancholy reflection when we meet
thousands of people on the Road, to think that there is
not among them a single person concerning whom we
can reasonably entertain the smallest Hope that he is
acquainted with the Grace of God in truth : But when
we look on the other side, we are constrained to say ;

" *What hath God Wrought ?* " Eighteen months ago we
should have been in raptures to have seen an Hindoo
eat at our Table ; now eating with us, is become so
common, that it is difficult to find room sometimes for
those who come. Nine Hindoos have been baptized,
of whom seven walk so as to be an honor to the Gospel ; and we expect to baptize an Hindoo and a Mussulman more before Capt. Hague leaves this place,
besides these four or five others are desiring to join our
Church, concerning whom we wish for a little more
satisfaction. They, however, appear to be seriously
enquiring ; and I doubt not, but they will be brought
forward in a little time. Some who have come and
rejected cast have returned again to their own relations ; and others have come several days Journey to
hear the word of God. Indeed, I have reason to believe, that a great work of God has been wrought
among us ; and trust it will continue, and greatly increase. Some among the Portuguese and Mussulman
are also enquiring, *what they must do to be saved ?*

Deism is very prevalent among Europeans here, yet
I have the greatest reason to believe that God is carrying on a Work among them. We have two Evangelical
Clergymen of the Church of England ; and I am much
mistaken if I have not perceived a more than ordinary
unction attending their Preaching lately. Several persons of great abilities have been brought decidedly to
trust in Christ; and to appear on his side.

Both myself and brethren are much delighted with the New York Mission Society. May the God of Abraham bless their efforts abundantly. If you see dear Brother Holmes or his colleagues give our very cordial love to them, and through them to the believing Indians. We shall be much gratified with anything curious relating to any of them, or indeed with only knowing their names. The name of the person who was our first-fruits unto Christ is Krishna, who has seen three others of his family received into the church, his wife, his daughter, and his wife's sister.

I must conclude, and indeed feel that I have tired you with this long detail. I thank you for the circular letter of the different associations. Do continue to send them, as they afford us much pleasure, and a knowledge of the state of the churches gives us a peculiar interest in them, and excites us to pray for them. Dear brother, pray for us, and especially for your very unworthy but

Affectionate brother in Christ,

WILLIAM CAREY.

CALCUTTA, June 15, 1802.

This last letter of Dr. Carey's comes with a strange force to those who read it after the lapse of so many years and with the knowledge of the events which have taken place since its writing. He who should, to-day, attempt to write the history of Christian missions, would scarcely think of looking to North America as the portion of the world in which to find a great ingathering of the church ; rather would he go to those barren fields of which Carey writes, and the very territory known to our fathers as the "Lone Star Mission" where, year after year, the word had been preached and the seed sown, but the laborer had seen no whitening harvest. Among the Telegus at Ongole and Nellore he would find ingatherings greater in one day than those over which Carey rejoiced as the result of a year's labor ; and yet as we read the letter we may almost catch the echo of a yet earlier account of a more ancient mission :

"Then tidings of these things came unto the ears of "the church which was in Jerusalem, and they sent "forth Barnabas that he should go as far as Antioch, "who, when he came, and had seen the grace of God, "was glad, and exhorted them all, that with purpose "of heart they would cleave unto the Lord, for he was "a good man and full of the Holy Ghost and of "faith."

They tell us that the days of inspiration are over, and that with the passing from earth of the last of the apostolic band there passed also the last lingering rays of that light else never seen on land or on sea, but, to some at least, it seems as if the Spirit which animated and energized the church at Jerusalem was the same ever-present and ever-potent Spirit which guided the councils and blessed the labors of the churches in England and America and far India in the days of Carey and his associates, and will in our day work the like results in the hearts and lives of men of like faith and like courage. The ingatherings in America, whose Pentecostal fervor and extent kindled the heart of William Carey in 1802, are the work of the same Spirit which in later years has gathered thousands into the churches at Ongole and Banza Manteke, and the interchange between home and foreign missions is, after all, but the refluent tide of a mighty ocean over which broods that divine Spirit, which at the creation moved upon the face of the waters, till from the darkness there came the light.

News did not travel as fast in the opening years of the century as it has done since the days of the submarine cable ; and it was not until 1802 that the English brethren seemed to have learned of the correspondence between Mr. Williams, representing the New York Missionary Society, and Dr. Carey ; but in that year the following letter was sent and received :

May 8th, 1802.

Dear Sir :—

We see by the Magazines you have had some correspondence with our dr Bror Carey at Serampore. A young man who is going with his wife to join them is obliged to go to New York to get passage. We recom-

mend him to your cordial friendship, as one whom we
think to be a partaker of the right missionary spirit.
Receive them, therefore, accordingly, my dear Bror,
and if they want any assistance in a pecuniary way,
you may be assured that Bror Chamberlaine's drafts
will be punctually paid by the Treasurer of the Society
in England.

They can tell you many particulars of the last news
from ye East Indies, as well as what concerns ourselves.   I must only subscribe myself in haste,

> Your cordial Bror,
> JOHN RYLAND.

To explain the allusion to Mr. Chamberlain, it is
necessary to travel back again to Olney and to the Baptist Church of which John Sutcliff was pastor there.
Mr. Sutcliff was not satisfied with confining his labors
simply to his pastoral office, but at his house (first that
of which the kindness of Mr. Wright has furnished a
view and later a larger edifice on the main street of
Olney), he had been in the habit of training young
men for the Christian ministry, and after the formation
of the Missionary Society, he trained not a few for the
Mission field.   Among the students thus trained by
him was John Chamberlain, formerly a farm-laborer of
Braunston, who had married Hannah Smith, a member
of Mr. Sutcliff's church ; and this is the " Bror Chamberlaine " alluded to in John Ryland's letter.   The

OLNEY.

East India Company, not satisfied with having banished
the missionaries from British territory in India, succeeded, by their influence, in throwing so many difficulties in the way of the embarkation of new missionaries
on British ships sailing direct for India, that it soon
became expedient for the missionaries to make their
way first to the shores of America, and from thence to
take vessels to India; and thus it happened that John
Chamberlain and his wife, instead of sailing from an
English port to India direct, came first to New York,
intending to sail thence for India; but it would appear
the city on the Schuylkill was in those early days a
more desirable shipping point than Manhattan Island,
and both for the sake of the continuity of the narrative
and as illustrating the minor difficulties that lay in the
way of missionary activity in those days, the following
letters are inserted:

PHILA., July 16, 1802.

DEAR SIR:

Yours of the 14th Inst. respectg Mr. Chamberlaine
came to hand yesterday. In the evening, I had a visit
from good Capt. Wickes, who informed me that he had
no thoughts of going to India himself, but that a vessel, a Capt. Davy, would sail from this port for Calcutta,
the beginning of next month. One of the owners concerned is Mr. Robert Ralston, a very religious man—
the Capt. and ship's company will probably be as is usual

—this Mr. Chamberlaine must expect. A worthy young man, a neighbour of mine, Dr. Robt. Davidson, is to go as Doctor and Surgeon of the Ship—by whom Doctor Staughton and myself propose writing to Messrs. Carey, &c. as the vessel is bound directly for Calcutta.

Capt. Wickes recd. some time ago a few lines from Dr. Fuller mentioning Mr. Chamberlaine, and means to interest himself this Day with Mr. Ralston, the Captain, &c. on his and Mrs. Chamberlaine's behalf— and will either this evening, or tomorrow inform me more particularly, when I shall again address you and let you know the result. The business is in good hands.

At present we are under some apprehensions of the yellow fever. It was brought to our City, the northern part of it, by the St. Domingo Packet. I hope God will be better to us than our fears and deserts. Should it prevail, I propose taking my family out of town, probably to Burlington, as Mrs. Rogers draws near the time of child-bed confinement. Should the fever prevail, of which you will be seasonably apprised, Capt. Wickes says that Mr. and Mrs. Chamberlaine need not enter the City, but take shipping at Chester, Marcus Hook, or New Castle, as the case may be. In all which country we have several Baptist friends, probably Mr. Chamberlaine may make it convenient to journey via Burlington. I am well assured that Dr. Staughton will be glad to see him, and I know, if I am fixed there, I shall.

Rev. Mr. Milledoler, for whom I preached last Lord's Day and of whose church Capt. Wickes is a member, is now in N. York on a visit. As he corresponds with one of our Missionaries at Serampoor, I am not sure which of them, I should like that he was introduced to Mr. Chamberlaine. Mr. Milledoler is an Evangelical Preacher. Religion appears to be on the revival among us and all around us. Oh, for greater effusions of God's Holy Spirit.

Very affectionately yours in a dear Redeemer,

WM. ROGERS.

PHILA., July 17, 1802.

DEAR SIR:

I wrote you yesterday morning by Post on the subject of Mr. and Mrs. Chamberlaine's passage to Calcutta. At noon good Capt. Wickes called on me again, having seen Mr. Ralston, Capt. Davy &c. They have agreed to take them on the following terms, viz; as the cabin will be occupied by the officers of the ship for sleeping,—the owners will cause a private room to correspond with the cabin by a door from the steerage to be fitted up for Mr. and Mrs. Chamberlaine as a lodging room and place of retirement, solely for their use; they are to eat in the cabin with the officers of the ship and to have free ingress and egress out of it whenever they

choose, the only exception being that of lodging.
The passage money must be paid before they sail,
400 dolls. *each*, and their names to be immediately
forwarded to Mr. Ralston, that is, provided they go with
Capt. Davy, in order that they may be entered on the
Role De Equipage.

You had better after this address Mr. Ralston altogether on the subject, as I shall probably be out of
Town, and Mr. Ralston having affectionately consented
to it.   Direct your letter thus,

Robert Ralston, Esq.,

Merch't.,

Philad'a.

I am credibly informed that Capt. Davy is a moral
and agreeable young man.   Our neighbor, Dr. Davidson, is generally esteemed so ; however, should anything occur on the passage of an unpleasant nature
there will be Mr. and Mrs. Chamberlaine's *own* room.

Don't you think, if they conclude upon going with
Capt. Davy, that they had better come on as soon as
convenient, at least as far as Burlington ; by stopping
there, they will learn the State of Phila. Dr. and Mrs.
Staughton will be glad to see them, and should the
fever prevent their visiting Phila. I can recommend
them to some of our Religious friends at Marcus Hook
or Wilmington.

I have taken rooms in Dr. Staughton's newly purchased house in Burlington, where I propose moving

my family in the course of a week or 10 days ; whenever in the course of providence I may meet with Mr. and Mrs. C. I will render them every assistance in my power.

The ship is to sail the very beginning of next month.

Capt. Wickes informs me that the passage from London to Calcutta is 100 guineas, so that something very considerable will be saved in going from Phila.

Very affectionately yours,

WM. ROGERS.

The following letters from John Chamberlain and Dr. Carey record the events of the voyage and disembarkation, both being dated March 2, 1803. After a somewhat detailed account of the voyage which would scarcely interest the reader, Mr. Chamberlain continues:

We had to beat up the Bay of Bengal against the Monsoon, which was rather tedious, but on the whole was in this respect very much favored. On the 20th of Janry. we took a Pilot on board and on the 22nd we saw the land, and going up the river we ran aground and were in a very unpleasant situation for three tides, the ship laying on her beam ends. We started all our water and on the 26th early in the morning we were afloat again without any damage. About 10 o'clock we had the joy to see Bro. Ward who had been informed of our arrival by a letter I wrote and sent by post and came down to meet us. About 10 miles below Calcutta we left the ship and accompanied Bro. Ward in his boat. Bro. Carey met us at the water's side, and took us to his apartments in the college where we were refreshed. The next morning we reached Serampore and were received by Bro. Marshman and the sisters with christian salutations. Brought to the conclusion of our voyage we thanked God and rejoiced in his goodness.

We rejoiced to find the work of the Lord prospers beyond our expectations. Two Hindoos, one a Brahman, and the other a Byragge were baptised a few days before our arrival, the other was baptised last Sabbath day week. Sixteen Hindoos have been baptised of which number 14 are church members. Of the other two, one is dead, and one is suspended. Our church consists of 27 members. Jehovah hath done great things, whereof we are glad. Last Sabbath day evening a Hindoo bror. spoke in the name of the Lord Jesus much to the satisfaction and astonishment of the Brethren. I did not understand him, but it gave me pleasure to see the desirable sight. This is the first time that a Hindoo has preached in such a public and regular manner. His discourse was nearly an hour long. His name is Petumber Shinge, an old man, of a very venerable appearance. God hath done great things in him, and it is our prayer and our hope that he will also do great things by him. We have assisted him in building a house at a place called Sook Saugor about 30 miles above us, where he has gone to live and to preach the words of life. God be with him. Our Bror. Krishna will, we hope, be very useful in the work of the Lord. His is truly a christian family. It may be said that he has a church in his house. All inquirers go to his house where they are entertained and instructed in the way of salvation. Our Bror. Krishna Persad, a young Brahman, gives us great hopes. May God raise up preachers from among the natives to carry on his work.

In Bengallee I as yet make very little progress. Being much engaged in the school I cannot attend to it so much as I otherwise should. If God preserves my life all that is very difficult will be soon overcome. I much like the Bengallee singing.

Now my dear brother farewell. Probably I may write to you again soon. May God bless you and yours. May the church prosper over which God hath made you an overseer. May you see it flourish. May the glory of the Lord be seen upon you and upon all the societies of the faithful in Christ Jesus in N. Y. and in all the U. S. Please to present my christian love to Doctor Rodgers, Messrs. Miller, Obeel, &c., &c. My dear partner unites in love to sister W., and hoping that God has helped her safely through and given you to rejoice in his goodness. Write to us often. Tell us largely of your welfare. Pray for us.

We rest,

Most affect'ly yours,

J. & M. CHAMBERLAIN.

SERAMPORE, March 10th, 1803.

6

My dear Bror.

I received your kind favour by the arrival of our dear Bror. Chamberlaine, who with his wife arrived here in good health to the great joy of us all. I trust that we shall find them to be real blessings to the Mission. The kind treatment which they received in America calls for our unfeigned gratitude. I trust that you are often remembered in our addresses to the throne of Grace.

Divine mercy is making large conquests in your favoured land, and I doubt not but you are all encouraged to labor with double ardor in the great work. I doubt not but many will speak evil of it, and perhaps there may be mixtures of human passions, and sympathies. Yet I most sincerely wish that such a work was taking place in India, and that we could see Brahmans, Mussulmans and Deists falling before the word of God.

I find that either success or want of it may prove a snare. For the first seven years of my being in this country my mind was often almost dried up by discouragement and want of success. I then felt spiritless, and went to the work like a soldier who only expects to be defeated. Since that more success has attended the work, and divine favour has compassed us about on every hand, yet I have remained in a most sinful, unmoved, dispirited and ungrateful. I have all along looked too much to myself instead of having my expectations wholly fixed on the Lord. I now see and lament my sin, but my soul is as it were confined to a prison and I find it impossible to feel, to hope, and to rejoice like others of the children, and ministers of the Lord. I trust you will pray to God in my behalf that I may be strengthened with strength in my soul, and that I may go in the strength of the Lord and make mention of his righteousness, of his only.

A most glorious work of Grace has been lately carried on near Cape Comorin in the Peninsula of India, 2700 have been baptised by the native ministers, besides about 1000 by Mr. Gericke, a pious missionary there, and all in the space of a few months. At present Bengal is a vast Wilderness, full of every thing hurtful, and discouraging, tho' not entirely without appearances of the Lord's gracious power. We have baptised 16 Natives, one of whom was afterwards murdered (I suppose by thieves). The word has had a wide circulation, and I think that the number of enquirers increases. We have people come to us from a great distance to hear about the way of Life, and [received] one on whom the Lord appears to have fastened convictions which we trust will end well. One man was baptised last Lord's Day and two a few weeks ago.

My many avocations oblige me to write short letters, and I am generally obliged to infringe on the hours of sleep to reply to the kind letters of my friends. I hope however that my shortness will not discourage

you from writing, or from writing long letters. I esteem the receipt of letters from my friends, as one of
the greatest privileges with which I am favoured by
the Lord. Send all the accounts of the work of God
that you can. This is an incumbent duty, being the
way by which you may strengthen the brethren. Love
to all your friends.

I am
Very affecty.,
Yours

WM. CAREY.

CALCUTTA, 2 March, 1803.

A correspondence having been now commenced with
members of the English Society, the exchange of
letters and news would seem to have become more
frequent, and the following letter from Dr. Ryland is
interesting as showing the difficulties attending trans-
port in the days of which we write. The "John
Cauldwell" referred to, if unknown to good Dr. Ryland, is abundantly familiar to the Baptists of America,
and we shall meet with him again in the history of this
movement.

DEAR SIR:

We have lately heard better news than ever from
our dear brethren in Bengal, with whom I find you
have been so kind as to correspond. It is a sad
disappointment, however, that no copies of the N.
Testamt. or even of so much as of the book of Matthw.

have yet arrived in England, except one sent by a private hand to Mr. Morris, which he sent to Edinburgh and I have one copy of a N. T. and two copies of Matth. given me by a gentleman who had bro't them from Inda for himself. 100 copies of the N. Testament were sent to a ship and receipts obtained of their lading, but the ship being too full they were return'd and buried undr. loads of goods at Calcutta for 10 months, then they were sent by way of America by Captn. Hague, but where Captn. Hague resides in America we have never been told, nor have we yet heard of the books. I rec'd. a letter lately from Bror. Carey, sent by America and so to Waterford in Ireland, on the outside of which was the followg. inscription. "New York Decr. 25, A packet is this day forwarded to you via Londn Your most obt. servt. John Cauldwell." But no mention was made of the *name* of the ship by which it was forwarded, nor have I ever heard of the parcel. These are very sad disappointments indeed. All this is of little int. to you Dr. Sir, but, if you know Mr. Cauldwell or Captn. Hague, I shall be extremely obliged to you to tell them how much I regret these misfortunes. May Grace, Mercy and peace be wth. you.

I am, Dear Sir,

Your cordl bror.,

JOHN RYLAND.

NORTH STREET, BRISTOL,
March 5, 1803.

The next letter from William Carey shows, in no small degree, the breadth of his mind and the universality of his sympathy. To most men the sphere of their own activities bounds the horizon of their hopes and of their desires ; but not so with the men to whom the race has owed its greatest debts of gratitude. With them, as with John Wesley, no parish can be adequate but the world ; and such a man was William Carey. Deep as was his interest in the progress of missions in Bengal, he abated no jot of interest in the progress of Christian work in other quarters of the globe, and his anxiety to learn of the success of the efforts of Elkanah Holmes among the North American Indians, and of the results of efforts to overthrow the slave-trade in the West India Islands, is no less indicative of the wide sweep of his observation than his warm tribute to the work of Mr. Gericke in another part of India and in connection with another mission is indicative of the extent of his Christian charity :

MY DEAR BROR IN CHRIST.

Having an opportunity of writing by the return of Mr. Smith and family to N. York, I can not let it pass without asking you how you do, and how affairs are going on in America at large, and at N. York in particular. Having at this time written to several correspondents at Philadelphia and other places in America all that I can say about ourselves can be only like the

dull repetition of a twice told tale. I shall therefore
be very short upon that head and enquire about the
American Missions. Do the Societies go on with courage? Are they countenanced by the public? Do persons fit for, and devoted to the work offer themselves
as Missionaries? How does dear Bror Holmes and his
colleagues? What success have they had among the
Indians? Is any thing done towards translating the
Bible into the different Indian Languages? Do the
Indians begin to attend to the duties of civilized life?
Are schools set up and well attended among them?
&c., &c., &c. I hope that the glorious work in the
Western and Southern States is still continuing, and
will continue. Are the impressions in general permanent or not? We are to expect that the blossoms
will prove abortive in many instances, but after every
production is not the Harvest great? What says the
World to this work? What say Infidels to it? I suppose they will scoff but cannot resist its evidence. Has
this glorious work spread into any more of the States?
Has it contributed at all to the destruction of that dis-
grace of America, and every civilized nation, the Slave
Trade? We have heard some time ago that the House
of Assembly in Jamaica has prohibited the instruction
of the Negroes, and their religious meetings. This is
a very lamentable circumstance, for there are many of
our Brethren there. It is undoubtedly the duty of us
all to wrestle hard with God in Prayer for their deliver-

ance. There can be no doubt but the hand of God
will fall heavily on those Islands whose trade and even
existence is supported by robbery, oppression, cruelty,
persecution and murder. The Lord will judge his
People, and when he maketh inquisition for Blood will
not forget the sighing of the poor and needy. I hope
and trust in God that the persecution of our dear
brethren there will not last long. May their persecu-
tors be converted and not destroyed.

We are all in health through the interposing goodness of the Lord our God, and the affairs of the Mission are in a promising state rather than otherwise.
The number of Natives baptised is twenty-six, two of
whom have departed this Life, and left a sweet savour
behind them. We have had some occasions to exer-
cise discipline, but upon the whole our friends give us
much pleasure, and we account them our Glory and
Joy. This part of the World has sustained a great loss
by the death of dear Mr. Gericke Missionary at Vapery
near Madrass ; he has been a Father in Israel for many
years, and his * . . . or rather the success of the
Gospel in the Southern parts of India has lately been
uncommonly great, and last year in a journey which
he made to the South he baptised and formed into
churches about 4000 persons who had then through the
instrumentality of native teachers and catechists re-

* Part of the letter torn away.

jected heathenism and embraced Christianity. About
a week before the account of his death arrived, letters
from him informed us that the work was still going on,
and that he was preparing for another journey to those
parts, but how wonderful are the Ways of God,—he
died Oct. 2nd last, and there is now no one to succeed
him. My paper is filled. Pray for us. Write to us,
and be assured of the Xn. Love of

Yours Affecty

WM. CAREY.

CALCUTTA, Nov. 15, 1803.

Before proceeding further with the correspondence,
it may be well to advert to the work of Elkanah
Holmes among the American Indians. A plain man
himself, and not gifted, as his correspondence seems to
show, with many of the graces of eloquence, Elkanah
Holmes yet had a marvellous power of winning his
way among the Indians of North America, and it
would have been well, indeed, for our nation could
most of its embassadors to the Indians have gone in the
spirit of Elkanah Holmes, and have met with the reception which he appears to have met. There is a
strange dignity and beauty in the following address
presented to Mr. Holmes in the name of the Seneca
nation, by Red Jacket, the celebrated Indian chief, on
Monday, October 20, 1800 :

" FATHER,

"We are extremely happy that the Great Good Spirit has permitted us to meet together this day. We have paid attention to all that you spoke to our ears at our last meeting. We thank the Great Spirit who has put it into the minds of the Great Society of friendship at New York to send you to visit us :—we also hope that the Great Spirit will always have his eyes over that Good Society, to strengthen their minds to have friendship towards the poor natives of this island. We thank the Great Spirit that he has smoothed your way, and has protected you through the rugged paths, and prevented any briers or thorns from pricking your feet. As you came on your way to visit us, you called on our Brothers the Oneidas, and Muhheconnuks, and Tuscaroras, who were well acquainted with you. We thank them for the pains they have taken in sending this good talk with wampum : (at the same time holding the talk and wampum in his hand) ; we are convinced that what they say of you is true, that you come purely out of love to do us good, and for nothing else ; and that there is no deceit in your business, or in the good people that sent you.

"Father, we now request you to speak something to us about Jesus Christ, and we will give attention."

He then addressed his people and requested them to give good attention to what Mr. Holmes was about to say, and make no noise, but behave in a becoming manner. Mr. Holmes then proceeded and endeavored to preach Christ to them. When he had concluded, Red Jacket arose and made the following speech to him, after consulting the chiefs :

" Father, we thank the Great Good Spirit above for what you have spoken to us at this time, and hope he will always incline your heart and strengthen you to this good work. We have clearly understood you, and this is all truth that you have said to us.

" Father, we believe that there is a Great Being above who has made heaven and earth and all things that are therein ; and has the charge over all things : who has made you Whites as well as us Indians : and we believe there is something great after death.

" Father, what you say about our loving the Great Spirit we know to be truth, as he has his eyes over all things, and watches all our movements and ways, and hears all we say, and knows all we do.

" Father, we Indians are astonished at you Whites, that when Jesus Christ was among you, and went about doing good, speaking the good word, healing the sick, and casting out evil spirits, that you white people did not pay attention to him and believe him ; and that you put him to death when you had the good Book in your possession.

"Father, that we Indians were not near to this transaction, nor could we be guilty of it.

"Father, probably the Great Spirit has given to you White people the ways that you follow to serve him, and to get your living : and probably he has given to us Indians the customs that we follow to serve him, (handed down to us by our forefathers) and our ways to get our living by hunting : and the Great Spirit is still good to us to preserve game for us : and Father, you well know you white people are very fond of our skins.

"Father, you and your good people know that ever since the white people came on this island, they have been always getting our lands from us for little or nothing.

"Father, perhaps if we had had such good people as you and your society, to have stepped in and advised us Indians, we and our forefathers would not have been so deceived by the white people ; for you have the Great and Good God always in your sight.

"Father, we repeat it again—we wish you and the good people of your society to make your minds perfectly easy, for we like what you say, and we thank the Good Spirit for their good intentions, and that they have sent you to visit us.

"Father, you do not come like those that have come with a bundle under their arms, or something in their hands, but we have always found something of deceit

under it ; for they are always aiming at our lands ; but
you have not come like one of those—you have come
like a father and a true friend, to advise us for our
good.—We are convinced that there is no snare in
your business. We hope that our talk to you at this
time will be communicated to your good society at
New York, and that the Good Spirit will protect you
and them in this good work that you and they have
undertaken—and we expect that the bright chain of
friendship shall always exist between us—and we will
do everything in our power to keep that chain bright
from time to time.''

Mr. Holmes seems to have given reports of his work
among the Indians not only to the New York Missionary Society, but to the New York Baptist Association,
in whose early Minutes many references appear to his
work ; thus in the Minutes for 1802 it is recorded that
an affectionate letter from the Mohheconnuk nation of
Indians at New Stockbridge was received, containing a
grateful acknowledgment of the reception of the books
sent them in the preceding summer ; and it was perhaps no unnatural outgrowth of this interest in the
work of Elkanah Holmes that, apparently in the year
1806, the New York Baptist Missionary Society was
formed and John Williams installed as its first President. In 1807 its membership is stated at 112 ; and
among its list of twelve Directors we note the name of

John Cauldwell, as to whom Dr. Ryland inquired. The receipts of the Society for that year amounted to $626.84, and it was resolved to employ a Missionary, a resolution which was carried into effect, the Rev. Charles Lahatt being appointed Missionary for the Society.

In the meanwhile the English Society was preparing to send out additional Missionaries, and their coming was announced in a letter from Andrew Fuller, the first Secretary of the English Baptist Mission Society.

BRISTOL, Dec. 5, 1803.

DEAR SIR :—

As four young men, and their wives and a child, are likely to be a while in your City in their way to Bengal, we take the liberty to recommend them to your brotherly kindness, persuaded from your former conduct towards our bror Chamberlain that you will willingly give them every assistance in your power.

Their names are Richard Marden, John Biss, William Moore, and Joshua Rowe. They and their wives are members of baptist churches, and have walked as becometh the gospel. Each of the young men has preached in our churches with good acceptance. They will advise with you, Mr. Collier, Mr. Jno. F. March, and Ezekiel Robins, Esqr., on whatsoever they may need advice. To these gentlemen we have been recommended by Dr. Rogers of Philadelphia. We will

JOHN WILLIAMS.

thank you to present our christian love and introduce our brethren and sisters to them.

They will show you their instructions, and be thankful for your advice and assistance in carrying them into execution ; especially in directing them to a suitable place or places during their stay in your City, where they might be at a moderate expense, and in the negotiation of a draft on the society.

Our Society will be much obliged to you and your friends for their assistance.

I am Affecy yrs.,

ANDREW FULLER.

All of the four named had been pupils of John Sutcliff in Olney, and were evidently warmly received by the friends of the Mission in New York. It is unfortunate that none of Rev. John Williams' own letters are in existence (as far as the editors are aware), and, consequently, the history of the New York days can only be conjectured. The young missionaries seem, however, to have made many friends during their stay in America, and many kind inquiries were made about them. From a short letter from Dr. Ryland under date of June 14, 1804, it would seem that the voyage from England to America must have been a long and, perhaps, dangerous one, and that apprehensions were felt as to their safety, for he writes : " I have but a few minutes time to write a line just to thank you and your friends for all the kindness you have shown to our dear Missionaries. The news of their safe arrival was like life from the dead, for we began to despair of ever hearing of them. May the Lord increase your usefulness and bless you abundantly." The same mail that brought this letter from Dr. Ryland must have brought a letter also from John Rippon bearing the same date, in which much interest is expressed in the mission of Mr. Holmes to the Indians, and indeed, this interchange of information as to the various forms of Christian work in which the correspondents on both sides of the sea were severally interested formed one of the strongest ties between the English and American societies.

The next letter in the correspondence is one from Richard Marden, written on the ship *Sansom*, off the Cape Verde Islands, and contains the narrative of his voyaging thus far. It is followed by a long and most interesting letter from Andrew Fuller.

SHIP SANSOM, CAPE VERD ISLAND,
July 4, 1804.

DEAR SIR :—

May grace, mercy and peace from God our Father and the Lord Jesus Christ be with you and yours continually. Most gladly do I embrace this opportunity of writing to you a few lines thus far on the passage, which I hope will not be in vain. Yesterday we made the Isle of Bonavista and passed it by. This morning about daylight we made the Isle of St. May ; we are now very near it. The captain talks of sending a boat ashore ; we are just within sight of St. Jago, where he talks of dropping anchor. I hope I shall be able to convey this to you from one of these Islands, but from which I am not yet certain. I have the happiness to inform you that we are all at present in the enjoyment of a good degree of health. We have none of us had any sickness worth mentioning. These light afflictions which are but for a moment will work out for us a far more exceeding and eternal weight of glory. There is nothing in this world worth living for. There is nothing desirable to the Christian in this land of the curse, this state of sin and imperfection. I wish to live only for God, to promote the interest of my dear Redeemer. How necessary is watchfulness and prayer in every step through life, but when I view my own short-comings, I have reason to be ashamed and confounded before God. I long to be delivered from the burden of sin, and to be sanctified, body, soul and spirit throughout. I hope, sir, that you and all my dear Christian [friends] will pray for me and for us all that we may be found faithful unto death. The work is great and arduous, and I feel myself weaker than a bruised reed yet through the help of God, I trust I shall be enabled to persevere even unto the end, and then when called to depart this life, I hope to be with Christ, which is far better. When I sat down to write, I little thought of saying so

7

much about myself and especially of running on in
this strain to such a degree, but you will excuse my
freedom. Tho' I am writing to an *Elder*, a *Superior*
and in one sense a *Stranger*, yet I am writing to a
Friend, and a *Brother*, for we are all one in Christ
Jesus.

The circumstances attending our voyage hitherto
are in general of a pleasing nature. We have had
good weather in general, except one heavy storm the
6th of June, about midnight. The Captain is quite a
gentleman. He behaves exceeding kind to us. We
have had preaching every Sabbath since we have been
out, sometimes once, and sometimes twice; we have
preached two or three times on deck on Lord's Day
mornings, the capn calls all hands to attend. We are
never hindered from attending to any religious duty.
We were likely to put back again to some port in
America a few days after we came out. The ship
sprung a leak, and they were obliged to keep the
pumps working every hour; this continued several
days, and the leak increased, but they found it out and
stopt it themselves. I must close; the boat is just
going ashore. I intend writing also to Mr. Smith, but
time will not permit, for which I am sorry. I 'll en-
deavour to embrace the next opportunity. Give our
kind love to all the dear friends in York, espy. to Mr.
and Mrs. Smith. As I have no opportunity of writing
to England, if you would write a few lines to any of

our friends the first opportunity, you would much
oblige, your humble servant,

RICHARD MARDON.

P. S.

While I was writing this, Mrs. Mardon wrote a few
lines to her friends, which I have taken the liberty to
enclose in this, which I would thank you to send to
England by the first conveyance.

KETTERING, Aug. 1, 180

MY DEAR BROR.

I recd. yrs. of June 12 a day or two ago.   We are all
greatly obliged by the kindness of our brethren in New
York to the Missionaries.   We feel it, and we rejoice
that others feel it a work which in all its operations
expands and unites the hearts of Xns.   We also rejoice to hear of the work of God in your country, tho'
some things attending it have rather stunned us ; but
in most instances of the kind there has been a mixture
of chaff among the wheat in order to try men.   I think
our churches (I mean the baptists) are low in general.
Those about the midland counties have suffered heavy
losses by the removals of Carey from Leicester, Ryland
from Northampton, Pearce from Birmingham, Morris
from Clipstone and Blundel from Arnsby.   These were
our most able and active ministers ; and though four
out of the five are labouring in other parts of the vineyard, yet the general connection hereabouts feel their

loss. I think the churches in the West of England
have been of late in the most thriving condition. An
Antinomian doctrine and spirit has almost ruined a
great number of our churches in Norfolk, Suffolk,
Yorkshire, &c.

We consider the mission to Bengal as the most favourable symptom attending our denomination. It
confirms what has been for some time with me an important principle, that where any denomination, congregation, (or individual) seeks only *its own*, it will be
disappointed, but where it seeks the Kingdom of God
and his righteousness, its own prosperity will be among
the things that will be added unto it. I have seen
great zeal for what among us is called *the dissenting
interest ;* and in such hands the dissenting interest has
died. Had they sought more to make men Christians,
they should in most cases have been dissenters of their
own accord. In fact I see that in those congregations
where the main object is what it should be, there religion flourishes. The same may be said of baptists.
If the first fruits of our zeal be laid out in making
proselytes to that denomination, however right the
thing may be in itself, the Lord will frown upon us and
leave us. But if we be mainly employed in making
men Xns, we need not fear but they will be baptists.
It is of great consequence to pursue things according
to their importance, making that a first concern which
is first, and that a Second which is secondary. In seek-

ing the salvation of others a man will find his own. He who is exalted as head over all things obtained that glory by denying himself for the sake of others.

I was delighted yesterday in reading some of our last intelligence from the East, down to Dec. 1803. A Dialogue founded on facts—drawn up with only a little variation in phraseology by bror Ward.

Boodheesa, one of the Xn natives was born a Mussulman and brought up to farming ; but afterwards became a Byraggee, a kind of holy beggar. Being instructed by his new Goroo, or teacher he left his friends and employment, and set off begging, and repeating the forms of his new cast. In this way he did many acts incredibly difficult and painful. Hearing a little of the gospel he came three days journey to Serampore ; heard more ; was inclined to wait for further instruction ; and was at length baptised, accounting all his hard-acquired holiness but "dung that he might win Christ and be found in him." On leaving Serampore he resolved to return to his house which he had forsaken on becoming a Byraggee. When he arrived he stood at the door, and as soon as they saw him they all with weeping invited him in. He told them he could not go in, as he had lost Cast, and he did not wish to give them sorrow without their consent.

"Come in my Son," said the Mother (a very old woman, weeping) "why do you stand at the door?"

Boodheesa. "No Mother, I cannot come into the house. You will lose your cast, for I have eaten with English people."

The Mother, brothers and wife. "Well, but cannot you come in?"

Boodheesa. "No, I will not come in, but if you will come and sit out, I will tell you what I have done, and why I have done it."

The Family. "Come then, let us go and sit in the Cow-house."

Boodheesa (sitting with his friends round him in the cow-house). "You all know that I have never done any thing but for the best. It was to seek my good that I became a Byraggee, and therefore you may be sure that what I have now done has been to secure my salvation."

Mother. "Well, my Son, let us hear."

Boodheesa. "You know that I have wandered up and down in search of the true way. I forsook the world. I became a Byraggee. I have obtained my food by begging. I have repeated the name of God continually. I have visited different holy places I have performed the Bromha Sadon.* I have performed the Soorja Sadon, and for 12 months, 12 hours every day fixed my eyes on the blazing orb, till I became blind, and my face, as black as ink, was dried up. You know

---

* Worship paid to Bromha.

that I then performed the Chundro Sadon * to recover my sight, and to obtain some fruit for my soul. Besides this, I have done other very severe and terrific acts, called holiness ; but all was in vain. I continued a slave to sin, and my mind was destitute of happiness. At length I heard of there being a new way preached at Serampore. I have been there, and have heard glad tidings, that Jesus Xt. came into the world, and bore the punishment due to sinners. This is a great word, and it has filled my soul with hope and joy. Hence I have laid aside the proud thought of making amends for my own transgressions. I make my refuge in his death, and consider all my own holiness as a heap of sin. I have been baptised in his name. If I can believe in him, and obey his command, I shall get over my everlasting ruin. If you can unite with me in becoming the disciples of Xt., then I shall find my home, my mother, my brother, my wife, and a Saviour all at once ; but if you cannot, then I will abide by my Saviour, and go every where proclaiming his name. If I die in this work, under a tree, or any where else, verily it shall then be well with me."

Mother. "My son, I am now become old. In looking round me I see only you and your brother and sisters. I see no world below but you. If you have

* The worship of the Moon, by fixing the eyes upon its shadow as seen in the water, and repeating a munter &c.

found this good news, well, Let your brother go with you and see and believe and if he find things so, and a Saviour has died for us, why may not we be baptised and share in your benefit?"

Sadutsa (the brother). "I will go to Serampore with you. I had thought of staying at home, and of remaining unmarried to nourish my mother till her death ; and then of becoming a Byraggee, that having left the world, at death I might obtain salvation. But now I will go with you, and hear about Yesu Khreest."

Mother. "Well, Son, let us go in. You must eat with us. Why should you stay out ? Are you then of a different cast from your own brother ? "

They leave the cow-house, and at the voice of maternal love, at the call of yr gospel, and in spite of the interdictions of the infernal cast, they eat and drink together, saying one to another, "Let us now go even unto Bethlehem and see this thing which is come to pass, which the Lord hath made known to us ! "

I have copied the above as a sweet morsel for you and the dear Xn. friends about you. I am obliged to you for your favourable reception of what I have written, and your wishes for me to write more. My hands are very full with Missionary labours. I have been out on that business the two last months. I believe our funds are now more than exhausted for the first time. But the bills from New York will be duly honoured. I have been lately preparing for the press an Octavo Volume of Expository discourses on the book of Genesis. It may however be a year ere it is out. It has been my practice to expound a chapter every Lds. day forenoon, for the last 14 years. This volume will be a part of those expositions. I wish I cd. get time to write Dr. Rogers. Remember me affectionately to Mr. Miller, Mr. Mason and all those dear friends, Smith, Cauldwell, &c., &c., whose houses and hearts were opened to our dear young people. We had many fears for them, but we bless God that hitherto he hath helped us.

I am

Yr. affecte. bror.,

A. FULLER.

This letter itself is a most remarkable one, exhibiting, as it does, two elements in the founders of this new mission which are seldom to be met, a wonderful breadth of view on the one hand, combined with a deep and clear insight into the character of individuals on the other. The churches have scarcely yet risen to an apprehension of the true spirit of Catholicity which breathes in the opening words of Fuller, and surely he would be a rash man who would lightly undertake to analyze with more of beauty and truth the feelings of the new convert than has been done in the simple dialogue with which the letter concludes, and which was

the work of William Ward, the third in the great trio
of the Serampore missionaries. Nor is the letter interesting only from the religious standpoint. The types
of Hindoo character presented in the dialogue, and in
many similar episodes from Ward's pen, are rapidly
passing away, and are being replaced by a strange
amalgamation produced by the mingling of Eastern
and Western civilization. Whatever else England has
done for India, she has not developed the native
character, and such examples of that character as are
to be found in this letter and in the pages of Ward's
famous work on the Hindoos are rapidly coming to
have a unique value as presenting a type of a civilization that has passed, or is passing, rapidly away.

It is to be regretted that the correspondence here
given contains but one letter from John Sutcliff, and
that a very brief and not a very important one. As it
is the only one, however, it is here presented to the
reader :

VERY DEAR SIR ;—

I seize an opportunity of sending by Mr. Harding,
a line to express my gratitude, and that of many here,
for your kindness to our young friends at New York.
Owing to a weakness in my right hand, I can write
but little ; but, perhaps, we could now and then exchange a line, an association letter &c., it would afford
me pleasure to receive any thing of this kind. Per-

ANDREW FULLER.

haps you may sometime have a friend coming to London, who would leave a small packet for me at the Rev. Mr. Button's, 24 Paternoster Row. Has any person defended the work in Kentucky, against Rankin's Review? Have seen Rankin, and should rejoice to see any judicious piece in defense of the work.

One of our friends mentions the kindness of a Mr. Whithington. If he ever lived in Manchester, I knew him, & Mrs. W.

With best wishes for your usefulness and comfort, I rest

Yours most cordially,

John Sutcliff,

Olney, Augt. 29, 1804.

The next letter in the series, from Joshua Rowe, one of the young missionaries who came out in 1803, takes up the narrative at the point where Mardon had left it. The good ship *Sansom* reached Madras in safety, and the letter records the fortunes of the little party after their landing, and with that from Richard Mardon himself, brings the narrative down to the close of the year 1805 :

Serampore, Octr. 3rd, 1805.

My dear bro. Williams :

Have just been informed by Bro. Marshman, who is come from Calcutta, that there is a ship going to sail for N. York in a few days. I suppose the shortness of the time alloted me will confine the limits of the present correspondence to one letter, and I am persuaded I owe that to you. Hope long before this my New York friends have received the profiles, &c. that I sent from Madras by the return of the *Sansom.* Many of them are a letter in debt to me. A few months since, I recd. some pamphlets, &c. from my friend, Mr. Cauldwell ; also, a share in a letter ! I had no idea, while in N. Y. that paper was scarce, if I had, I wd. have left him a quire.

From the supposition that our letters from Madras have been received, I shall say nothing respecting our voyage in the *Sansom.* During our residence at Madras, we experienced much kindness from Europeans. We had an opportunity of preaching, in the house in wh. we lived, every Lord's Day, and often on week days. In general, we were pretty well attended. Hope the seed sown will take root. Some of us were invited to stay. They went so far as to make three subscriptions, one to help defray our expenses while there, another to build a Chapel, and another for a standing fund, the interest of which was to go towards our support if we would remain ; some individuals also came forward with considerable offers, on condition of our continuing. These circumstances had much weight on my mind, being solicited to stay. After considering the design of our coming out, and also of there being a Mission already established there, we answered their solicitations in the negative.

Am sorry that I have but little to say respecting the flourishing state of religion at Madras. The death of Swartz and Gerick will be severely felt. They were truly apostolic Missionaries. There are two Missionaries here, Mr. Paezold and Dr. Rottler (from Tinquibar). From all I cd. see and hear, money is the great idol of the former, but the latter (Dr. R. of Tinquibar) I sincerely love as a Missionary. Hope the Lord will raise up more faithful servants, and thrust them forth into his vineyard.

We had to wait a long time for a passage, and after all were obliged to leave Brethn. Mardon and Biss behind. About the 4th of Feby. last, Bro. Moore and self sailed for Bengal, and in about 15 days arrived at Calcutta, after a narrow escape from a French Frigate.

We found our friends here well, except the affliction occasioned by the death of Mrs. Chamberlain. Am very happy in my present situation. Have my hands full of work, which is so various that I cannot here particular mention them. Since my arrival, Bro. Carey has baptized 10 persons, 3 of whom were natives and 2 Europeans. Expect that Bro. Carey will baptize 4 or 5 more, next Lord's Day. Bro. Moore has been to Dacca to distribute tracts. Bro. Biss is going to live near Dinegapore, and Bro. Mardon is going into the Jassore country. There is a chapel going to be erected by subscription in Calcutta, for the use of all who preach. Bro. Carey continues at the college. Is publishing a Sanscrit Grammar and Mahratta Dictionary. The Brethren have engaged, under the patronage and support of the Asiatic Society and College Council, to translate and print some of the Hindoo Shasters. The Ramyun is the first selected, and will take 3 or 4 years to accomplish. Hope the Bible will soon be completed in the Bengalese. The translation of the scriptures into several of the eastern languages is also going on. We have had two or three inquiries within this day or two. Petumber Singe is dead ; he died triumphing in God. Most of our native brethren give us much pleasure. Many of them preach. Upon the whole, we have much reason for thankfulness.

Am glad to hear of the increase of your church. Often think of you, often pray for you, often anticipate the meeting above. Brethren and Sisters, did they know I was writing, would cordially unite with Mrs. R. and self in love to you, Mrs. W. and all our N. Y. friends.

Most affectionately yours,

JOSHUA ROWE.

It is not for want of a will that I have not written more. I am in hope of giving you a little more by Mr. Cauldwell. Hope you will write me the first opportunity.

SERAMPORE, Decr. 26th, 1805.

REVD AND DEAR SIR :

A fair opportunity now presents itself to send you a little news from India which I can by no means let slip. I wish I had time to write more of my friends in New York, but I must beg to be excused for the present.

Two of our Brethren, J. Maylin and J. Fernandez, Junr, Esqrs, who are members with us in full communion, have taken a passage in the *William Penn* of Philadelphia on their way to England, and expect to sail in the course of a few days. They intend at present to travel from Philadelphia to New York in order to procure a passage direct to Bristol ; it is probable, therefore, that you will receive this letter at their hands. As they are both entire strangers to America, it would be of great service to them to know where to light on a Christian Friend. Provision of this kind, however, will be made by some of the senr Brethren who are writing to different Friends in America, and I believe to you. Should you, or any of the Friends of Christ in New York be favoured with their company I think you will not only find it pleasant but profitable, as they will be able to tell you many particulars of the state of affairs in this part of the globe, and especially what the Lord has done for us, and for his church in this place. And indeed we may say with the Psalmist, " the Lord hath done great things for us, whereof we are glad." 'T is true, when we look around on the multitude that our eyes are called daily to behold who are involved in heathen darkness and superstition, bowing down to idols and trusting in gods that cannot save, there is enough to make our hearts ache, and to excite every tender emotion of the mind ; but, on the other hand, when we reflect on the success with which the Lord has crowned the Mission, we have reason to rejoice and shout for joy. I don't know how many Hindoos have been baptised and joined our Church from the first, but since our arrival at Serampore, in May last, I suppose about 30 have joined us. We had the pleasure to see 10 in one day publicly avow their attachment to the Redeemer by being baptised in his name. A pleasing sight ! The Lord will carry on his work in spite of all opposition. He is making inroads in Satan's Kingdom. It begins to totter, and must finally fall, for Christ must reign till he hath put all enemies under his feet.

The Lord has blessed several of our native Bren with ministerial gifts, and others are promising. We have a Missionary Station at Cutna, about 90 miles to the north, superintended by Bror Chamberlain. Bror Fernandez, senr, who resides at Dingapore, is publishing the gospel in that neighborhood. We expect him here in a few days. Bror Biss is going with him. We have several native Bren at Jessore, more to the east. We have taken some steps towards forming a station there, which we hope soon to accomplish. I expect to reside there. I am sorry I have neither time nor room to enlarge, but I hope this defect will be supplied by our Bren. We are all well and happy. Mrs. M. unites in love to you and Mrs. W. with all our Xn Friends.

I remain yours in the best of bonds,

R. MARDON.

By the kindness of Sir W. T. Lewis we are enabled to present also a letter addressed to the English Society by six Missionaries and giving a more general account of the work at Serampore.

DEARLY BELOVED IN OUR LORD

Considering you as being one with ourselves, and as equally sharing in our sorrows and our joys, we feel a pleasure at the return of the Season for our quarterly correspondence. We have reason to complain a little, on account of not regularly receiving your quarterly communication. Twelve months, if not more, have elapsed since we received the last public letter from you; notwithstanding that the Fleet, and many extra ships, have arrived from England.

It is our desire to impart every thing interesting; altho' when we view the vast importance of the work in which we are engaged, the many circumstances, which have occurred, and the disqualifications we possess, when compared with the greatness of the under-

8

taking, we are constrained to impart anything of a pleasing nature, with fear and trembling.

As a family, God has laid us under great obligations, by his tender dealings towards us. The greater part of us have been laid under his afflicting hand. Bror. Biss has an attack of the Liver Complaint

He has undergone one salivation, and is now entering upon another ; we hope he has received much benefit from the first and that this will effectually remove the complaint.

As a Church, we have been exercised with various feelings. We have been under the painful necessity of excluding John, Golamee and Anunda for conduct unbecoming the Gospel. Our Brother Seeboo of Jessore died in April last. He was at his own house among his heathen relations, therefore we know but little, respecting the state of his mind at the hour of dissolution. Our Brother Bykunta was at his house a short time after his death. His widow told him that a few days before her Husband's death, he refused to repeat the names of the Heathen Gods, when desired to do it by some of his heathen neighbours.

He recommended it to her to embrace the Saviour and expressed his desire that she would go to Serampore to be instructed in the way of life. May God seal this, his dying advice upon her heart as we trust he did that of our departed Petumber Sing. Our native Brethren & Sisters at Ram Krishnoopore, have had to encounter much opposition, and some of them are now reduced to very destitute circumstances. When we behold the Christian fortitude which they have manifested in the midst of their distress, we are constrained to acknowledge that the Hand of God is with them.

Amidst all our painful exercises, we are refreshed by pleasing occurances.

We have felt happy in being enabled to restore Roop, Mohun, and Goluk Mohun's wife, to church fellowship. Mrs. Ephraim Burford whose father is a member of the church under the Pastoral care of Mr. Booth; Ram Nul an Hindoo from Mirzapore; Dazee; our Bror Rogunath's wife; Mohun a carpenter, who now lives at Serampore; and Manick of Jessore, have given themselves up to the Church.

With respect to the Mission in general many things have occurred, which afford us much encouragment. At Present we have four enquirers, Bhyrub a person from Krishnonagoi Punshanum from the district of Mahmoodshye; Ram Yeebum from Calcutta, and Saneteram from Chitagong.

There is much in them of a pleasing nature, and we hope that the hearts of some of them are turned unto the Lord.

Several other persons have occasionally visited us.

These circumstances tend to establish our faith in that precious promise, "The word of the Lord shall not return void."

Our dear Bro' Fernandez still continues abounding in his labours of Love, and is not without hope that the Lord is owning them for good.

The Lord seems to have begun to work in the heart of a Mussulman, who lives near Dinagepore, whose name is Turrickulla. Bro' Fernandez sayes, in a letter lately received from him that he still continues to give him hope. " When ever he comes to see us he joins us in family prayer. He lately demolished an Eedgah" (a wall with steps along one side of it on which people sit to read the Koran) built many years ago upon his own little Estate.

By this act, and his inclination to the Christian Religion, he has raised some enemies. The school is still continued. Our native brethren Galak and Futick, are gone to Dinagepoor, and from their present activity, promised to be useful in making known the word of Life. Bidya-nath left us with them but has deserted them and we fear has deserted the cause too. Krishnoo Pawl also accompanied them for the purpose of itinerating about Guamalty, Malda Ragmahl &c. He was kindly received by our European friends at these places, and his labours seem to have been very acceptable. He has now returned.

Bro' Chamberlain has had many opportunities of

preaching the word & distributing tracts to numbers of people from different parts of the Country. He gives us a pleasing account of Kangalee, whose assistance is very useful to him when itinerating. He has some hope respecting a person of the name of Seeboo Roy, who has been to see him several times and manifests a concern about the Gospel. Kangalee has been to visit Grididor who we fear is gone back into the world. He was very ill, but seem to have little concern about his soul.

The people at Cutwah are much prejudiced against the Gospel, in consequence of which, several of the most promising children have been taken from the school.

Several of our Jassore brethren are now at Serampore. Krishnoo has taken a journey thither to enquire into their state and to preach the word to them. He found some of them very low, being much discouraged on account of the opposition they have met with, since the Gospel has been more generally made known there.

The school at Bishoo Hurry is for the present given up. Krishnoo returned with an enquirer or two.

Our English Congregation at Calcutta continues in nearly the same state as usual. A piece of ground is purchased in a populous part of the city, for the purpose of erecting a Chapel. At Present a temporary place is erected for preaching in Bengalee.

Our Bro' Juggunnath is stationed there that he may converse with people and distribute tracts.

Our brother Krishnoo Dap of Ram Krishnoopore, is also engaged in Calcutta in the same work.

Great numbers of natives flock to this place. The Purchase of the ground has nearly exhausted the subscription. We hope the Lord will provide.

We have had opportunities of circulating tracts, pretty extensively. Two of us with some native brethren, have been at a large assembly of natives at Sooksanger, met for the purpose of worshipping Gunga. Great numbers received the tracts with apparent eagerness, and many swam after the boat for them, when they came away. We have also distributed a considerable number at the annual resort of the people, to the idol Zuggunath, near Serampore. Some of the Brahmans, and others who are influenced by them, tear the tracts which they have received, to pieces, and throw them about the road ; but we rejoice in the hope, that many of them are carried away by those who may perhaps read them, and pray that the blessing of God Almighty may attend them.

Proposals have been sent to different parts of this country, and published in the Newspapers, for translating the Scriptures into the Shanscrit, Bengalee, Hindoostanee, Persian, Mahratta, Guzerattee, Orisa, Carnata, Telinga, Burmah, Assam, Bootan, Tibet, Chinese, and Malay Languages. About 15 thousand rupees have been subscribed for this purpose, which is lodged in a bank at Calcutta.

We need your Councils your prayers, and your effectual support; and we assure ourselves that you ever bear us upon your hearts. May the best of Blessings return into your own bosoms !

If God pour out his spirit "this wilderness will soon become a fruitful field. The little one shall soon become a thousand and the small one a strong nation."

On this rests all our hope.

> Dear Brethren
> We remain Yours
> In everlasting bonds,
> W CAREY
> J. MARSHMAN
> W WARD
> J BISS
> W MOORE
> J ROWE
> F. CAREY

SERAMPORE,
June 24th, 1806.

A short letter from Richard Mardon and another general letter to the Society are also placed before the reader (the latter by the kindness of Sir. W. T. Lewis), being the record of the Mission up to the summer of 1807.

SERAMPORE, Decr. 16, 1806.

MY DEAR SIR :—

Once more I embrace an opportunity to tell you what is doing, and how the Lord is dealing with us in this part of the world. He has of late tried us, and is indeed still trying us in various respects. But this we know, that what he does is always best; he is too wise to err, and too gracious to be unkind. The greatest trial at present is the restriction of our labours among the natives. We are shut up and cannot go forth. The great men seem to be afraid that evangelizing the heathen will alienate their hearts from them. Did they know what true Christianity means, they would be of a very different opinion. I trust the Lord in his providence will soon open a way for the more universal extension of the word of life among these dark and benighted nations. The work is his, and he will carry it on in his own time and way. For this let us earnestly pray. O Lord, let thy kingdom come!

Bror Biss has for a long time been under the afflicting hand of God with a complaint of his liver. Various means have been tried for his recovery, but hitherto without effect. He is now in Calcutta under the care of Dr. Hare. His opinion is that the only remedy which Bror Biss can take for the preservation of his life, is his removal to a colder climate, and that his remaining in Bengal another hot season would terminate his life. We are, therefore, using all diligence to procure a passage for him and his family to England. Bror Moore is now in Calcutta for this purpose. The most probable mode of conveyance will be by way of America if we can procure a passage by any of the American ships that are now in port. You may probably see him once more in New York. If so, he will be able to give you more intelligible information of the state of this Mission, perhaps, than any of us could do by writing a whole volume. This is a great affliction to us both as it respects the loss of our Brother's usefulness in this country, and also the heavy expense that will fall upon the Mission in sending him to England, which under present circumstances, must sink us very low. However, we must submit to the will of God, and we ought to do it cheerfully.

Notwithstanding these things, we have abundant reason for thankfulness for the privileges we enjoy. The work of the Lord is still going on. Several of our native Bren are itinerating in different parts of the country, making known the word of life, and Bren Carey, Marshman and Ward are busily engaged in translating and publishing the Scriptures. When this is accomplished, India will enjoy a blessing indeed. May the Lord teach the inhabitants how to prize it. There is a spirit of hearing and inquiry manifested in different parts of the country. We have 2 or 3 native bren in the neighborhood of Malda, who preach to great multitudes and the natives solicit their attend-ance.   I visited that neighborhood last summer with 2 native brethren, and was much encouraged.

Bror Chamberlain is labouring abundantly about Cutna, and there is reason to hope not without success. At Calcutta, the face of things wears a very pleasing aspect.   We intend as soon as an opportunity offers, to make an attempt to send the gospel into the Empire of Burmah.   Bror. Chater and I are appointed to engage in it.   We are now waiting for a conveyance.   The Lord has lately sent several eminently pious and zealous ministers of the church of England into this country, in which we greatly rejoice.   He will carry on His work.   The perusal of the most recent accounts that have arrived of the state of religion in America gratified me very much.   I long to see more.   Mrs. M. unites in love to yourself, Mrs. W. and all our kind friends in N. Y.

I remain, yours affectionately, &c.

R. MARDON.

To the Society

SERAMPORE, *June* 25th, 1807.

VERY DEAR BRETHREN.

With pleasure we embrace an opportunity of renewing our quarterly correspondence, & of communicating to you a few things which have taken place among us since our last.—— We are still called upon, as in times past, to mingle our prayers & our sorrows with yours.   We do not as yet behold any remarkable outpouring of the Spirit nor many instances of conversion to God, yet we trust that the work of the Lord is going forward in some degree among us.

In the course of the last quarter 7 persons were added to the Church by baptism. On the 5th April 2 Natives were Baptized, Fukeerehund, a person who came hither from Sadhkalee in the District of Krishneenagur, & Bhanumutty sister to Futeek, who is a member of the church at Dinagepore. On the 3rd of May were baptized 5 more, 4 of whom are members of one family residing at Calcutta, Mr Derozia, his wife & 2 Daughters. They have a long time attended the preaching of the Gospel there. Mr and Mrs Derozia are far advanced in years. The other person is a Mr Oakey, sergeant in the army, who resides in Fort William. His father was a member of the Baptist Church at Kingstanley near Stroudwater in Gloucestershire.

Bror. Chamberlain has also baptized 3 persons at Cutna one of whom is a Koolin brahman, who has 14 wives, Vindyabon, a Byragee, & Kangalee's sister.

April 4th. Neeloo & Unna who had been several months under suspension were again restored to Church fellowship. Neeloo has since then been excluded.

May 3rd. We were under the painful necessity of excluding Bhyrrel & Bhagvat for improper conduct.

April 20th. Three Brethren, Ram Mohun, Konnie, & Kristno Dass were set apart to the office of Deacons.

May 31st. Ram Mohun was set apart to the work of the ministry

Our Bror Balukram, after a lingering illness, which he seemed to bear with much resignation, quitted these mortal shores on the 13th inst. & we trust is arrived safe in glory.

April 20. Our Bren. at Jessore formed themselves into a church, & appointed Sheetaram & Koobeer to the office of Deacons. At present they have no pastor— Since the formation of the Church, Kristno and Ram Mohun have visited them alternately, and administered to them the ordinance of the Lord's supper. They must necessarily, under present circumstances be visited monthly by some Bror. from Serampore.

Brother Fernandez has lately made a preaching tour into the northern parts of Bengal. He preached in several large villages and markets. "Many people" he says "heard the word with great attention." He intended to extend his circuit to the Boundary of the British Dominions, but as some parts of country are much infested by robbers he was persuaded to return. He intended, after his return to take another tour for about a fortnight but was prevented by sickness. His last letter informed us that he had been very ill but was recovering. May the Lord prolong his life to a very distant period, for much usefulness in his Church.

In our last letter we informed you of the Departure of Bren. Mardon & Chaler to Rangoon, for the sake of ascertaining the practicability of forming a Mission Station there. We have now to inform you of their return to Serampore. They left Rangoon April 17th & arrived here May 23rd. They obtained a passage, free of expense, by a ship belonging to two European gentlemen at Rangoon. Their report relative to the object of the Mission, particulars of which have already been sent to England, encourages us to hope that the Lord will open a door for the Introduction of the Gospel into that Empire.

Bror. Wm. Carey, Junr and 5 Native Brethren Kristno, Kristno Dass, Sebukram, Jagernaut, & Govendhar returned from an itinerant journey to Malta on the 9th of April. In almost every place which they visited the people came crowding around to hear the word of life, and very often some went away much affected. In the course of their journey they visited Mudnabatly, also Serasing & the neighbourhood around. On their return, they stopt several days at Cutwah, & accompanied Bro. Chamberlain to Augradweep, a place where he laboured abundantly to introduce the Gospel. They spent two days there in talking to the people & met with a little opposition —— Only Kristno and Sabukram accompanied Bror. William to Malta. The other 3 Bren. had been itinerating in that neighbourhood some time before.

A Petition has lately been presented to Government signed by 116 of the inhabitants of Calcutta for permission to erect a chapel there for the use of Protestant Dissenters which was granted. The walls of the Chapel are raised ready to receive the roof. In the course of a few months we hope it will be finished and opened.   Our American friends have given us a fresh instance of their liberality, and of the interest which they feel in the diffusion of Gospel light among the Heathen, by sending out an additional supply 2,400 dollars to forward the oriental translations.

To-day we have received an account of the arrival of 5 boxes from England.

This dear Brethren is the substance of what has taken place among us in the course of the last 3 months. O that we could tell you of Multitudes of the Heathen crying out "Men & Bren. what shall we do?"   We long to see a *Pentecost* but we must wait the Lord's appointed time.

Dear Bren. pray for us.   Pray that the word of the Lord may have free course in India.   We need your prayers and all the help that you can render us.

    We remain

        Dear Brethren

            Yours in the Gospel of Christ,

                W CAREY

                J MARSHMAN

                W WARD

                R MARDON

                W MOORE

                J CHATER

                J ROWE

                WM ROBINSON

                F CAREY

P. S. When Capt Wickes was here he mentioned accidentally to Bror. Ward his having incurred a considerable loss by the laying in of stores for our Bren. Chater & Robinson &c. as what he had charged the Society did not reimburse him. Though this was mentioned in free conversation without the view of obtaining anything from the Society yet we thought that Capt. Wickes had rendered too many services to the Mission of Bengal for us to be willing that his family should suffer thereby.

We therefore pressed him to give us an account of the extent of his loss, but we could by no means prevail upon him, & we were at last constrained to give up pressing him further, after getting him to promise that he would make known the thing to the Society, viz, we suppose if you press him to it.

We leave these facts with you knowing that your feelings & ours towards this dear man are the same.

Revd. A. FULLER,

Kettering,

Northamptonshire,

England.

The next letter written by Ryland, in the summer of 1807, serves to present one effect of Christian missions which is, perhaps, not as often dwelt upon as it might properly be,—the strong bond that it furnishes between Christian nations united in missionary effort. Already the mutterings of war were heard, and while it was not

till 1812 that the resort to arms was actually had between England and America, not a few in both countries were eagerly fomenting the growing discontent;
but among those who, like John Ryland and John Williams, were chiefly concerned for the extension of the
reign of Him whose chosen title was "The Prince of
Peace," no prospect of war between Christian nations
could be anything but saddening, and far as their
effort and influence went, the bonds of union were
strengthened.

28th Augt., 1807.

DEAR SIR:

A young man called on me this week, who says he
is a member of your Church, and enquired if I had any
thing to send to you or other friends at New York, and
tho' I am now uncommonly hurried by some extra
business, I was unwilling to let him go, without sending you a line. I hope the work of the Lord is going
on in your neighbourhood, and other parts of the
United States; and I pray God to prevent any discord
from taking place between the two countries. All
war is dreadful; but especially that between Protestant
States, and above all between people sprung from the
same stock, and united by so many ties as ought to be
felt between Englishmen and Americans. But, alas!
we are all miserable sinners, and the God has raised
up in both countries many who begin to feel as saints,
yet they themselves are imperfect, and have but little

influence in regulating the concerns of nations. We can only sigh and cry for the madness of others around us, and pray God to check their selfish passions, and inspire them with an abhorrence of bloodshed. Well may the whole Creation wait with earnest expectation for the manifestation of the sons of God, in hope that the Creation itself shall be delivered from the bondage of corruption in the glorious liberty of the Sons of God. How is every part of this visible universe now abused by the sin of man! and how little do even the Children of God look at prest like what they *should* be, or even like what they *shall* be, in the latter day of glory. We are much obliged to our American Brethren for their generous co-operation in favor of our East Indian Mission, and the kindness shown to those who have passed by the way of the United States to Serampore; as well as for their late kindness to poor Mrs. Biss. May the Lord abundantly reward them, for what they have done for disciples in the name of disciples of Jesus. We are just planning a mission to Jamaica, where some coloured Brethren have been useful to a considerable degree, but are exposed to great oppression for want of having any European to take their part. I have this week heard of a renewed attempt to deprive them of all liberty of conscience, by a most iniquitous and oppressive ordinance of the Magistrates of Kingston, but we hope our Government will interfere again in their favor. We apply'd,

9

a year or two ago, with some good effect, and obtained the disannulling of an act of the Assembly. But the prest attempt is much worse than the former.

Brother Fuller was here about 3 weeks ago, at our annual meeting, when he preached the sermon before the Education Society, and spent about a week with us. A remarkable work of grace has been going on at Beckington, about 20 miles off, under the Ministry of a very worthy man of the name of Hinton. Great additions were made to his Church last year, and many more are under concern since.

But we seldom seem to fish with a net, as you have often done in America. It is very uncommon, I mean, for an awakening to seem to run through a town or a village. The most singular case to those I have read of, in your country, was the awaking at Sheepshead in Leicestershire near 30 yrs. ago, when my dear friend Guy was first settled there. We s'd. bless God, however, that his work goes on at all. Oh that it may extend itself widr. in every direction, both here and with you. Wishing much of the presence and blessing of our adorable Lord,

I remain, Dear Sir,

Your cordl Bror.

JOHN RYLAND.

As the correspondence of the Serampore missionaries with the churches generally in America increased, the number of their letters to those who had been first their only correspondents, of course, diminished ; and during the years between 1809 and 1812, but few letters seem to have been received by Mr. Williams. Three of these, from Dr. Carey, Joshua Rowe, and John Chamberlain, respectively, furnish the narrative of events at the mission station of Serampore during those years. Bnt that the interest of the churches in America had not flagged is shown by the fact that in 1810 still other missionaries arrived from England, making their way to India by way of the United States, and brought with them commendatory letters from Andrew Fuller. Of this little group of mission-aries, Messrs. Johns and Lawson, with their wives, and a Miss Chaffin, no very full record is now obtainable. One, at least, of them, Mr. Lawson, seems to have been, for a time, a student under Sutcliff at Olney, but of the rest of the party no definite information has been re-ceived. The three letters, therefore, above referred to, must serve as the record of these years.

MY DEAR BROR.

I recd. yours by our Brethren who lately arrived here in safety from America. A letter from you is always to me a welcome treat, and I therefore hope you will not be sparing in your correspondence, even though I should prove but a poor correspondent in return. I am sure that if you rightly judge of my engagements you will easily pardon a short letter, and if you rightly judge of my wants, you will always favour me with a long one.

I have written repeatedly to different correspondents in America nearly all that concerns the present situation of the Cause of our Redeemer in India, and scarcely know what to add, as scarcely anything new has turned up since I wrote my last letter to America. Small, and feeble as our Redeemer's interest in this country now is, we have the greatest reason to rejoice in what the Lord has done. I believe the number baptized this year in our churches amounts to fifty-six, and by the end of the year I trust it will be about sixty. There are five churches now organized in Bengal, and one in the Burman Empire, and two stations occupied where churches are not yet formed. One of them is on the borders of Bantan, and formed for the express purpose of introducing the Gospel into that country. A Brother is going in a few days to carry the word of life to Oorissa. In short we have the utmost reason for encouragement, and for further exertion in the cause of our Lord Jesus.

The translation and printing of the word of God goes forward as fast as it can reasonably be expected to do. The entire Bible is printed in the Bengalee language, and a second edition of the Pentateuch is in the press. In Sangskrit the new Testament is printed, and the old Testament nearly to the end of Exodus.

In the Oorissa language, the New Testament, one vol. of the old Testament, viz, Job. Canticles is printed, and to about the XL. ch. of Isaiah of the next volume. In Hindoothannes, the N. Test. is printed to the 1 Epis. of Corinthians, and the whole Bible translated, except the Pentateuch, and from 1 Kings to Esther. In the Mahratta language the New Testament is printed to Acts IV, and the translation of the whole Bible considerably advanced. The whole N. Test. is nearly translated into the Chinese language and I expect that the gospel by Matthew will be printed by the end of the year. The whole of the Chinese scriptures must be printed by wood plates, and not by moveable types like other languages ; of course the labour of engraving these plates is very great. We have twelve workmen constantly employed in this department alone. The whole N. Test. and part of the old are translated into the language of the Sacks, and the printing in that language is begun. The whole N. T. and part of the old are translated into the Telinga language, and into the Thurnata, but the printing is not yet begun. It is necessary for you to know, in order that you may estimate the difficulty of this work, that there is a different character used for each of these languages, except one, so that we have to cast types for all of them, and except in two or three instances our types are the first ever cast for these languages, so that we have not only the languages to acquire in a critical and grammatical manner, but we are also obliged to attend to every letter and even to the minutest stroke in each letter. We have to fix the orthography of each language on rational and grammatical principles, and to correct all the errors which copyists make, who have no rule of spelling but their own fancy.

We began about three years ago to print the N. Test. in the Gosjeratti language, but relinquished it on account of some circumstances which then turned up. The copy lies by us, but the printing has not yet been resumed. The translation into the Burman language is begun, but the printing has not yet commenced; it probably will be soon begun, as we have cast types in that character. To these we hope soon to add the   language.

My paper is expended, and my time gone, excuse my abrupt conclusion. Pray for us, and believe me to be

Very affecty yours,

W. CAREY.

CALCUTTA, 7 Decr. 1809.

SERAMPORE, Dec. 19th, 1809.

MY DEAR BROTHER WILLIAMS:

I received yours of May last by brother Gordon; and beg you to accept my warmest thanks for the soul reviving information it contained. The intercourse between this and America has been suspended so long, that it is quite a treat to receive a letter from you. I

often think of my dear friends at New York and feel
the savor of those happy moments I have spent in com-
muning with them. We have received the liberal con-
tributions made by our friends at New York, on account of the translations, and feel exceedingly thankful
for them. The prosperity of the church of which you
are the pastor, gladdens my heart. Give my warmest
love to all who are the members of it. If I could go to
New York as easy as I can go to Calcutta, I should
certainly indulge myself with the pleasure of spending
next Sabbath day with you ; but since this cannot take
place, let us be looking forward to the time when we
shall meet in the realms of eternal days. It is time for
me to have done with these expressions of affection
towards you, and go on to a subject in which you will
feel yourself more particularly interested.

You have no doubt heard of what has taken place in
England, relative to Missions ; as also the impediments
we have met with in this country. I am happy to
inform you that these things, which to human appearance were insurmountable, appear rather to have forwarded the cause than to have impeded it. It is easy
for God to bring good out of evil. It was principally
owing to these impediments that we thought of sending a Mission to Rangoon in the Burman Empire.
Brethren Chater and Felix Carey are settled there.
God has hitherto favored them in a remarkable manner. Those in power have shewed them much favour.

They have built a Mission house and a number of European traders who reside there, have subscribed something handsome towards defraying the expense. They have made considerable progress in the language, and expect soon to send us something to print. Although that Government is exceedingly arbitrary, yet it tolerates all kinds of religion ; and those who are public teachers of any religion are allowed privileges which are denied even to those who fill high stations under Government. There is no cast among the Burmans, they will eat or drink with an European and are devoid of many of those prejudices which so much fetter the natives of this country. Upon the whole, our brethren are greatly encouraged to go forward, and surely, we have reason to hope that God will abundantly bless their undertaking. Remember them in your addresses to a throne of grace. It is a matter of great thankfulness that God has sent his gospel to this populous country. The cause of Christ prospers in Bengal. We are extending our missionary exertions, and God is from time to time, adding unto his churches. Oh! that they may be such as shall be saved with an everlasting salvation. About 57 have been baptized this year, at Serampore, Calcutta, Dingapore, Goamalty Jessore and Berhampore. Twenty-seven of this number were baptized at Berhampore, and belong to His Majesty's 22nd Regiment which is now lying at that military station. These persons had long formed a religious society, and were at length convinced of the truth of believers' baptism by reading their Bibles. When they found that Brother Chamberlain, whose station is a day or two's journey from Berhampore, was a Baptist, they solicited him to baptize them. At first, by the influence of a clergyman who resides there, their head officer interfered, in consequence of which their baptism was postponed for some time; but at length they have been permitted to follow their Lord in his appointed way. Bro. Chamberlain often visits them; he is now gone thither, and expects to baptize two or three more. There are two or three among them who have gifts for public speaking, and when they have no other means, they give a word of exhortation. It is a pleasing thing to see so many pious men in a Regiment of Soldiers. Would to God there were so many in every Regiment. We have an Armenian brother settled in Jessore. He has lately been set apart to the work by the laying on of hands. In the course of the last six weeks, he has baptized several natives. Last Ordinance Sabbath, he administered the Lord's Supper to eleven persons besides himself. Many are inquiring respecting the gospel in Jessore, and I hope God has a great work to do there. In Bheerboom several of the natives have renounced their gods, and are enquiring about Christ and his salvation. May the Lord lead them in the right way. Brother Mardon is still at Goamalty. Some months ago he met with much encouragement, but now the interest there is very low. He has baptized several, two or three of whom, we

hope, have died in Jesus. One or two have left him, so
that at present the church there is in a low state. It is
a delightful thought that God can and we have reason
to hope, will revive his work there. Brother Moore has
been sometime at Miniary, but is now on his way to
Bankipore, near Patna. He intends setting up a school
at this place as a means of supporting the station.
Brother William Carey, Junr. resides at Sadamahl, near
Dingapore. Brother Carey has the happiness of having
two of his sons missionaries. Oh ! that God may raise
up the three boys which he has given me to be pillars
in his church, when I am laid in the silent grave. We
are just going to send Brother John Peter, a member of
the church at Calcutta into Orissa, as a missionary.
Since we opened the chapel at Calcutta, which was in
January last, the congregation has doubled. Many
have been added to the church, and others are coming
forward. A few months ago, brother Carey was dan-
gerously ill ; but blessed be God he is now perfectly
recovered.

I have only time to add that Mrs. Rowe unites in
love to you, Mrs. Williams, and all the dear, dear
friends at New York.

I am, My dear brother,

Most affy. yours,

J. ROWE.

P. S.

I enclose you a specimen of our translation. The
brethren have forwarded a number of these works to

Dr. Staughton, to send to you. They beg you, when you have gratified your friends with a sight of them, to present them to any public body you may think proper. The same works have been sent to Doctors Staughton, Rogers and Baldwin, for the same purpose. You will therefore, please to be careful not to present them to any to whom the other gentlemen send them. We have also sent to Dr. Staughton a Memoir containing an account of the progress of our translations, and the monies received and expended, which you will no doubt see.

Since writing the above, Bro. Ward has recd. a letter from Bro. Chamberlain, by which we find that he has baptized nine more of the soldiers, in the 22nd, and that there are 3 others seriously examining the subject.

SERAMPORE, Octr. 28th, 1812.

MY DEAR BROR.

It is a long time since I wrote to you. Your affectionate letter, which came to hand a few months ago reminded me of my great neglect of a very kind friend. But apologies are useless.

I thank you for your remembrance of me. I am not worthy of your notice, but the work in which I am engaged is worthy of all honour. I have not forgotten my dear Brethren and Sisters at New York; I have frequently rejoiced to hear of your prosperity. Blessed be the God of all grace who has kept you as his own people and gladdens you with success in his work.

You have heard of my leaving Bengal and of my

going to Agra.   This will inform you of my removal
thence and of the probability of my settling again in
Bengal.   I was sent down under an arrest by orders of
the Government, but on what account, I know not.
Government gives no accounts of matters.   A word is
law here without any assigned reason.   Had I by any
imprudence brought this upon myself, I should have
been distressed, but being conscious of innocence, my
heart has rather exulted in this unfavorable event than
been discouraged by it.   When will the rulers of the
earth be wise ?   In this country they are exceedingly
jealous of that which would be their stability, and
foster that, which, if God do not graciously prevent
will, it is very probable, be their overthrow.   Nothing
is opposed in this country but true Christianity.   Hindoos
may burn their poor women, drown one another, bury
one another alive, with impunity, if not with approba-
tion.   Musselmen and Hindoos have their temples and
mosques supported by the Government, and Roman
Catholics are assisted and permitted to do what they
please.   A drunken, proud, tyrannical man, or a
whoremonger may be a chaplain to their stations, but
a Protestant missionary is to be driven about, and sus-
pected of everything that is wicked, and the pious and
zealous clergyman is persecuted and despised.   Yet
blessed be God, truth triumphs in the midst of these
unfavorable circumstances, and we rejoice in hope of
seeing its success more abundant, and more conspicu-
ously glorious through the opposition which it meets.

At Agra, we had much family affliction. Our three children were removed from us by death, but we have abundant cause to praise the Father of mercies for his goodness to us. We had a pretty school and a small congregation of Europeans to which I preached, and I hope not in vain. Just before our departure, I baptized one and had we continued, probably some more had been baptized before this time. There were several respecting whom, we have a pleasing hope that the Lord Jesus has been manifested to them, through the Holy Spirit's blessing on the means of grace. The translation of the New Testament into the Hinduwee, I was enabled to begin, and the four Gospels are nearly finished for printing, and a great multitude of the natives heard the word of salvation. Our journey, we hope, will not have been in vain, in which many parts of the N. T. were distributed in many places, and many people heard the gospel. A missionary has this to encourage him that in the cause of Truth no great effort shall be lost. Its success may not be apparent, but it shall have its weight in the opposition to the cause of the Evil One.

I have spent many a pleasant half hour with our new Bren. and Sisters, whom the good hand of God has brought to us, in conversing about America. We are glad to hear of you and your prosperity. Remember me affectionately to my kind friends Smith and Caldwell and Broughton, who, I am informed is with you. It would have afforded me much pleasure to have had a line from him and his family. Present my thanks to them for their former kind regards to me. I shall be much gratified to hear from them frequently.

I would most cheerfully fill this sheet, were I not quite jaded with letter writing. Present my love to your Bren. in the Gospel who may have known me. Mrs. C. unites in regards to your spouse. Peace and prosperity attend you at home and abroad.

I am,

Yours in the bonds of the Gospel,

26th Octr.   J. CHAMBERLAIN.

President Madison's war message was sent in June 1, 1812, and on the 18th of June war was declared with Great Britain. All the efforts of those who, on both sides of the sea, had deprecated war were in vain, and the inevitable conflict came ; but even the actual existence of hostilities could not destroy the bands which knit together the hearts of those united even by a more sacred tie than that of country ; and in the very month of October, when Decatur was winning his victories on the ocean, and those who spoke the same language and sprang from the same mother-stock were waging fierce warfare, William Carey, at Serampore, was writing to John Williams in New York a letter which was to be the signal for a new campaign of peaceful but more glorious conquest, in which England and America, no longer foes, were to be generous rivals.

My Dear Bro.

It is a long time since I wrote to you; My numerous avocations must be my apology, and indeed this apology is the true one, for want of will is not the cause; I shall however now write you a short note to make amends for my long silence and request a continuance of your correspondence.

You as well as myself are acquainted with the circumstance of five Brethren having been sent from America to begin a Mission in the East, they have all safely arrived at this place, Gov't however have absolutely refused to let them stay here, and have peremptorily ordered them to leave this place and not to settle in any country belonging to Great Britain or her allies; We have tried our interest, but have succeeded no further than to gain permission for them to go to the Isle of France, to which place Bro. and Sister Newel went before the arrival of the other three, It soon appeared that the mind of Bro. Judson had been much employed upon the subject of Believers Baptism, and in a little time after his arrival he and Sister Judson wished to be baptized, with which we complied, and they were accordingly both baptized publickly at Calcutta in the name of the blessed Trinity. I enquired of Bro. Judson what could have induced him to take this step; to which he replied that on his voyage he thought much on the prospect of meeting with us at Serampore: He knew that we were Baptists, and supposed that he might probably be called to defend infant Baptism among us. This led him to examine the evidences for it; and the further he proceeded in this examination, the clearer the evidence for baptizing believers only, and that by immersion, appeared. He frequently conversed with Mrs. Judson upon the subject, which was the occasion of her thinking as he did upon that ordinance. Since his baptism he preached a very excellent discourse upon the Ordinance, which We intend to print, with an account of the change in his views in his own words.

Since his baptism I hear Bro. Rice has been thinking closely upon the subject and to night I was informed that he had made up his mind to follow our Lord in his Ordinance. He disputes the matter with his other Brethren, and it is difficult to say what will be the effect of his conversation.

Now what is to be done with these Brethren? They expect to be discarded by the board of Commissioners for Oriental Missions. We shall advance them temporary supplies but we are not able to invite them to become Missionaries for this Baptist M. society without first writing to England and receiving our Brethren's consent. Our Brethren Judson and Rice would also be glad to be American Missionaries.

Can not our Baptist brethren in America form a Missionary Society either Auxiliary to our Society in England, or distinct from it, as may appear most eligible, and take these Brethren as their Missionaries? I believe they are men of the right stamp. They intend to settle eventually on the Island of Java, but must go first to the Isle of France on account of the orders of Government. One of our Brethren is also going thither, viz to Java. We will them with advice, and every thing else within our [power.]

I think this circumstance opens a new scene of Duty to our Baptist Brethren in America; and though I am persuaded that their proper sphere of action is among the Indians of North and South America, and in the West India Islands, yet this extraordinary call should not be lightly passed over.

The Lord is still enlarging our borders, about [persons] are now expecting to join the Church at Calcutta and to be baptized in a month or two more.

Calcutta.   I am
    20th Oct.r 1812   very affect.ly yours
                                    W. Carey.

In June, 1810, Adoniram Judson, a young theological student at Andover Seminary, had, with a few of his associates, prepared a memorial which they presented to the Association of Congregationalist ministers meeting at Bradford, in Massachusetts. In this memorial they asked the advice of their elders in the ministry as to their own engaging in the work of foreign missions, and, as a consequence of the memorial, the Board of Commissioners for Foreign Missions was formed ; and on the 19th of February, 1812, Messrs. Judson and Newell, with their wives, sailed from Salem, Massachusetts, for Calcutta, to be followed by Messrs. Hall and Nott, with their wives and Mr. Rice, who sailed from Philadelphia on the 24th of the same month. The story of that eventful voyage is best told in Dr. Carey's own words :

MY DEAR BROTHER :

It is a long time since I wrote to you. My numerous avocations must be my apology, and indeed this apology is the true one, for want of will is not the cause. I shall, however, now write you a short note to make amends for my long silence, and request a continuance of your correspondence.

You as well as myself are acquainted with the circumstances of five brethren having been sent from America to begin a mission in the East. They have all safely arrived at this place. Government, however, have absolutely refused to let them stay here, and have peremptorily ordered them to leave the place, and not to settle in any country belonging to Great Britain or her allies. We have tried our interest, but have succeeded no further than to gain permission for them to go to the Isle of France, to which place Brother and Sister Newell went before the arrival of the other three. It soon appeared that the mind of Brother Judson had been much employed upon the subject of believer's baptism, and in a little time after his arrival he and Sister Judson wished to be baptized, with which we complied, and they were both baptized publicly at Calcutta in the name of the blessed Trinity. I inquired of Brother Judson what could have induced him to take this step, to which he replied that on his voyage he thought much of the prospect of meeting with us at Serampore. He knew that we were Baptists, and supposed that he might probably be called to defend infant baptism among us. This led him to examine the evidence for it ; and the further he proceeded in this examination the clearer the evidence for baptizing believers only, and that by immersion, appeared. He frequently conversed with Mrs. Judson upon the subject, which was the occasion of her thinking as he did upon that ordinance. Since his baptism he preached a very excellent discourse upon the ordinance, which we intend to print, with an account of the change in his views in his own words.

Since his baptism I hear Brother Rice has been thinking closely upon the subject, and to-night I was informed that he had made up his mind to follow our Lord in his ordinance. He disputes the matter with his other brethren, and it is difficult to say what will be the effect of his conversations.

Now, what is to be done with these brethren? They expect to be discarded by the Board of Commissioners for Oriental missions. We shall advance them temporary supplies, but we are not able to invite them to become missionaries for the Baptist Mission Society without first writing to England and receiving our brethren's consent. Our brethren Judson and Rice would also be glad to be American missionaries.

Cannot our Baptist brethren in America form a missionary society, either auxiliary to our society in England or distinct from it, as may appear most eligible, and take these brethren as their missionaries? I believe they are men of the right stamp. They intend to settle eventually on the Island of Java, but must first go to the Isle of France on account of the orders of government. One of our brethren is also going thither, viz, to Java. We will give them advice and everything else within our power.

I think this circumstance opens a new scene of duty to our Baptist brethren in America; and though I am persuaded that their proper sphere of action is among the Indians of North and South America, and in the

10

West India Islands, yet this extraordinary call should not be lightly passed over.

The Lord is still carrying on his work, about twenty persons are now expecting to join the church at Calcutta and to be baptized in a month or two more.

I am very affectionately yours,

W. CAREY.

CALCUTTA, Oct. 20, 1812.

But a few days could have elapsed after the receipt of this letter when the following overture was received from the brethren in Boston :

BOSTON, March 23, 1813.

DEAR BROTHER :—

By the arrival of the Reaper in this port, last Saturday, from India, letters have been received from several of our friends in Calcutta, particularly from Mr. and Mrs. Judson, Dr. Marshman and Mr. Rice. The latter, like Mr. Judson, has been constrained to examine the subject of Christian baptism, and has come to the same result. He was not baptized on Oct. 22, but expected to be soon.

This change of sentiment, he has stated (as he informs us) to Dr. Worcester, the Secretary of the Board of Commissioners for foreign missions. He has also concluded by the advice, or in concurrence with the Baptist brethren at Serampore, to go with Mr. Judson to the Island of Java. Dr. Marshman and both of the above brethren unite in urging the formation of a Baptist mission society in this country, in order to take up those brethren, and direct and support them independently of our English brethren, or as an auxiliary to the Baptist society in England.

Dear brethren, the events which have taken place in relation to the foregoing missionaries, are highly interesting and important. The voice of divine providence in them seems loudly to call for our speedy attention and assistance. We have already two societies formed, as you will perceive by the accompanying circular, which have this objective view. But, dear brethren, we want your advice and assistance. We would gladly engage all our churches throughout the United States in this great work of sending the preached gospel among the heathen. The difficulty seems to be, in part at least, to fix upon a proper plan. Can you devise and propose any plan for forming an Executive Committee, with sufficient power to carry into effect our united efforts? There must be somewhere a common center, a general treasury into which all the money in whatever way raised may flow. We have no anxiety whether this deposit should be in Salem, Boston, New York or Philadelphia, provided we can only fall upon a plan that will unite all hearts.

The society in Salem have already collected more than $500, and have voted one-half for the support of Mr. Judson and the other for the translation.

Our infant society in Boston has almost without any effort received subscriptions to the amount of nearly $400. It will soon be increased, no doubt, to several hundreds more.

Will you, dear brethren, give us your advice on the following points, viz:

1. Will it be best at present to request our Baptist brethren in England to take these young men under their patronage and to consider us only as an auxiliary society?

2. Shall we attempt to appoint and support them ourselves; if so, who shall appoint them?

We cannot doubt but the subject must impress you in a similar manner as it does us, and hence hope for your cordial co-operation. We hope your late efforts in raising money for repairing the loss at Serampore by the late fire will not discourage you in the present undertaking, as we will most cheerfully advance the first necessary installment. We are, dear brethren, very respectfully yours in the gospel of a precious Saviour,

THOS. BALDWIN,
LUCIUS BOLLES,
DANL. SHARP.

To

 Revd. JNO. WILLIAMS,
  " JNO. STANFORD,
  ARCHIBALD MACLAY,
  DANIEL HATT,
  CORNELIUS P. WHYCOFF.

With this letter closes our narrative of the inception of missions among the Baptists of America. The succeeding steps in the formation of the Triennial Convention, which has developed into the Baptist Missionary Union, are matters of familiar history and need no further repetition here ; but a word or two of review may not be out of place.

Perhaps to the cultured reader who has glanced through the letters here presented, the prevailing feeling will be one of astonishment at the simplicity of the men who wrote these letters, and at the unostentatious character of those who received and acted upon their suggestions. Certainly, it was a plain, almost an illiterate, company who inaugurated this mighty movement ; but we have no farther to seek than to the little band of Galilean fisher-folk to find the elements of power and of permanence. Of the work of those first eleven, it was said that, when their enemies " perceived that they were unlearned and ignorant men, they marvelled," and it will not be strange if such marvelling should be aroused by the boldness of others who, in later days, had learned the same lesson with Peter and John, and, like them, " had been with Jesus." Without great resources, without the advantages of education, save as it was gained by slow and painful self-culture, without the influence of friends, except as they were won by the example of noble and self-sacrificing lives, without the patronage of the great, and in the face of the opposition, not only of the infidel and the scoffer, but also of the nominal church, these men wrought their work for God and for humanity. There was no glamour of romance about their lives ; the homes from which they came were peasant homes— "apostates from the loom and renegades from the anvil," their courtly critics called them ; and even when the patient industries of their lives had won for them something more of rank, the associations of their early days were still called up in taunting scorn. "Was not Dr. Carey once a shoemaker ?" said a young British officer, who had just met him at a social gathering in India. "No, sir," said Dr. Carey, quietly turning on the questioner, "only a cobbler." But it was this very power of simplicity and readiness to accept just the station and just the portion which their Master had assigned them, that gave to these modern Apostles their power, and that gave to their work its permanence ; and from the simple story of their lives comes back to us that refrain of mingled rebuke and encouragement which the prophet heard from the angel's lips : "Not by might nor by power, but by my spirit, saith the Lord of hosts."